SEMITIC STUDY SERIES

EDITED BY

RICHARD J. H. GOTTHEIL and MORRIS JASTROW Jr.
Columbia University. University of Pennsylvania

SEMITIC STUDY SERIES
EDITED BY
RICHARD J. H. GOTTHEIL and MORRIS JASTROW Jr.
Columbia University University of Pennsylvania

N⁰. IX.

SELECTED BABYLONIAN BUSINESS

AND

LEGAL DOCUMENTS

OF THE

ḪAMMURABI PERIOD

BY

ARTHUR UNGNAD, Ph. D.

OF THE ROYAL MUSEUM AT BERLIN

WIPF & STOCK · Eugene, Oregon

Wipf and Stock Publishers
199 W 8th Ave, Suite 3
Eugene, OR 97401

Selected Babylonian Business and Legal Terms of the Hammurabi Period
By Ungnad, Arthur
ISBN 13: 978-1-60608-381-9
Publication date 01/08/2009
Previously published by Brill, 1907

To my friend

HERMANN RANKE

PREFATORY NOTE.

In publishing this part of the Semitic Study Series embodying a selection of the business and legal documents of the Ḫammurabi period, the editors beg to announce that three other parts covering similar documents (*a*) of the still older period of Sargon and the Ur-dynasty (*b*) of the neo-Babylonian period and (*c*) of the Persian period are in preparation by Messrs. LAU, UNGNAD and CLAY respectively, and they hope also to arrange for a volume on documents of the Cassite period.

August 1907.

INTRODUCTION

The study of the early Babylonian business and legal documents was inaugurated by the publication of about a hundred texts falling within this category by J. N. Strassmaier [1]). These tablets had been discovered by W. K. Loftus at Tell-Sifr near the ancient town of Larsa (now Senkereh), in the southern part of Babylonia. They belonged to the reigns of Nur-Ramman, Rim-Sin, Ḫammurabi and Samsu-iluna. The style and writing of these documents offered considerable difficulties, so that it was necessary to wait for more material, before a better understanding of the contents could be expected. This material was gained through purchases made by Dr. E. A. Wallis Budge who, on his travels in Babylonia, acquired for the British Museum a large number of old Babylonian business documents (1888). A thorough study of these tablets enabled B. Meissner to prepare a volume [2]) which must be considered the groundwork of all further researches concerning this

1) *Die altbabylonischen Verträge aus Warka* (*Verhandlungen des fünften Internationalen Orientalistenkongresses.* Zweiter Teil, pp. 315—364, pl. 1—144), Berlin, 1882.

2) *Beiträge zum altbabylonischen Privatrecht* (*Assyriologische Bibliothek*, Vol. XI), Leipzig, 1893.

subject [1]). MEISSNER edited and translated 111 texts — including a number of tablets which, in the meantime, had been purchased for the Royal Museum at Berlin — and he collated and used for comparison many others which he did not publish. On subsequent journeys Dr. BUDGE obtained several more collections, and in 1896 a splendid edition of these, together with the old material not yet published by MEISSNER, was begun by TH. G. PINCHES in the *Cuneiform Texts from Babylonian Tablets etc. in the British Museum*, Vol. II. Other parts containing the same kind of texts soon followed: IV (1898), VI (1898), VIII (1899). Since that time little was added [2]) until 1906, when H. RANKE edited [3]), in excellent autograph copies, 119 documents of the Ḫammurabi-dynasty together with translations of some of them.

Nearly all the documents of the Ḫammurabi period

---

1) A little earlier TH. G. PINCHES edited a few tablets of this period in his work: *Inscribed Babylonian Tablets in the Possession of Sir Henry Peek*, London, 1888.

2) V. SCHEIL, *Une Saison de Fouilles à Sippar* (Cairo, 1902), contains a catalogue of a great part of the tablets discovered during an exploration of the ruins of Sippar which was carried on by the Turkish government (1894). The old Babylonian texts not yet embodied in SCHEIL's work were published by TH. FRIEDRICH (*Altbabylonische Urkunden aus Sippara* in *Beiträge zur Assyriologie*, Vol. V, part 4), Leipzig, 1906, whose edition of the texts, however, as well as his attempted translations must be used with caution.

3) *Babylonian Legal and Business Documents from the time of the First Dynasty of Babylon* (*The Babylonian Expedition of the University of Pennsylvania.* Series A: *Cuneiform texts.* Vol. VI, part. 1), Philadelphia, 1906. A list arranging all the old Babylonian business documents hitherto edited according to their contents will be found on pp. 13—16 of this work.

hitherto published, except those found by LOFTUS, were drawn up at Sippar in the north of Babylonia. Other places, however, have also furnished contracts and legal documents of the same period, as e. g. Nippur, Larsa, Dilbat, Kiš.

Among the treatises based upon the published texts we have to mention those of PEISER [1]), PINCHES [2]), DAICHES [3]), MEISSNER [4]) and SCHORR [5]). The dates contained in these documents have been made the subject of special study by LINDL [6]) and KING [7]). The dates belonging to the reigns of Ammiditana and Ammiṣaduga will be treated by the author on the basis of a recently discovered chronological list belonging to the Royal Museum at Berlin [8]). A valuable treatise on the

---

1) F. E. PEISER in SCHRADER'S *Keilinschriftliche Bibliothek*, Vol. IV, pp. 8—49.

2) TH. G. PINCHES, *Some Early Babylonian Contracts or Legal Documents* (*Journal of the Royal Asiatic Society*, London, 1897, pp. 589—613 and 1899, pp. 103—120).

3) S. DAICHES, *Altbabylonische Rechtsurkunden* (*Leipziger Semitistische Studien* I, 2), Leipzig, 1903.

4) *Aus dem altbabylonischen Recht* (*Der alte Orient* VII, 1), Leipzig, 1905; and *Theorie und Praxis im altbabylonischen Recht* (*Mitteilungen der Vorderasiatischen Gesellschaft* X, pp. 25—71), Berlin, 1905.

5) M. SCHORR, *Altbabylonische Rechtsurkunden aus der Zeit der I. babylonischen Dynastie* (*Sitzungsberichte der Kais. Akademie der Wissenschaften in Wien; phil. hist. Klasse*, 155. Band, 2. Abhandlung), Wien, 1907.

6) E. LINDL, *Die Datenliste der ersten Dynastie von Babylon* (*Beiträge zur Assyriologie*, Vol. IV, pp. 338—402) and F. DELITZSCH, *Randbemerkungen zu Lindl's Abhandlung*, *ib.*, pp. 403—409.

7) L. W. KING, *Letters and Inscriptions of Hammurabi* (cf. p. X, note 4) Vol. II, pl. 217 ff., Vol. III, pp. 211 ff.

8) A. UNGNAD, *Die Chronologie der Regierung Ammiditana's und Ammiṣaduga's* (in *Beiträge zur Assyriologie*, Vol. VI, 3).

personal names of this period has been published by RANKE [1]).

An important aid in the study of these early Babylonian business documents is the famous Code of Ḫammurabi, discovered 1901/02 by the French expedition at Susa [2]). This incomparable document of ancient civilisation must be used as the basis for all philological investigations concerned with the language [3]) of the Ḫammurabi-period [4]). It must be noticed, however, that

---

1) *Early Babylonian Personal Names* (*The Babylonian Expedition of the University of Pennsylvania,* Series D, Vol. III), Philadelphia, 1905; cf. also RANKE's thesis: *Die Personennamen in den Urkunden der Hammurabi-Dynastie,* München, 1902.

2) V. SCHEIL, *Code des Lois de Ḫammurabi* (*Mémoires de la Délégation en Perse,* Tome IV) Paris, 1902.

3) Cf. the author's treatise: *Zur Syntax der Gesetze Hammurabi's* (*Zeitschrift für Assyriologie,* Vol. XVII, pp. 353—378; XVIII, pp. 1—67).

4) A great many letters also have been found which constitute either *a*) private documents, their language resembling that of the business documents and which have been studied by B. MEISSNER, *Altbabylonische Briefe* in *Beiträge zur Assyriologie,* Vol. II, pp. 557—564, and M. W. MONTGOMERY, *Briefe aus der Zeit des babylonischen Königs Hammurabi* [Berlin thesis], Leipzig 1901; or *b*) letters from the king; their language being the same as that of the code and which have been edited with a translation and commentary by L. W. KING, *Letters and Inscriptions of Ḫammurabi, King of Babylon* (three volumes), London, 1898—1900. Cf. also F. DELITZSCH and J. A. KNUDTZON, *Briefe Hammurabi's an Sin-idinnam* (*Beiträge zur Assyriologie,* Vol. IV, pp. 88—100; G. NAGEL, *Die Briefe Hammurabi's an Sin-idinnam, ib.,* pp. 434—483, and F. DELITZSCH, *Zusatzbemerkungen zu Nagel's Abhandlung, ib.,* pp. 483—500. — The historical inscriptions of the same period have also been treated by KING, *Letters* etc. To a different division of the literature belong the old Babylonian omen-texts translated by J. HUNGER, *Becherwahrsagung bei den Babyloniern* (*Leipziger Semitistische Studien* I, 1), Leipzig 1903.

the language of the contracts, sometimes written by careless or even unintelligent scribes, shows much less accuracy than that of the code which seems to have been composed by the best scholars of the time. But on the other hand, the language of the business documents has this advantage over that of the code, in that it affords us an insight into the spoken language of the period. The blunders committed by the scribes can only be explained on the assumption that the vernacular language differed somewhat from the written one, so that a scribe who had not mastered the intricacies of the language might easily overlook a rule which was no longer observed by the people, but to which a better educated man would pay due regard.

As the texts contained in the following collection are intended to introduce the student into the study of the early Babylonian contract-literature, I have not hesitated to give emendations wherever I suspected an error in the edition or on the tablet itself; for the same reason I have restored the texts when incomplete. The student who desires to consult the original [1]) editions, is referred to the following list [2]):

1) The tablets belonging to the Royal Museum at Berlin (Nos. 18, 19, 31) I was able to collate myself.

2) Abbreviations: CT = *Cuneiform Texts from Babylonian Tablets in the British Museum;* MAP = B. Meissner, *Beiträge etc.* (v. p. VII, note 2); R = H. Ranke, *Babylonian Legal and Business Documents etc.* (v. p. VIII, note 3).

1. = MAP 96,	Bu. 88 — 5 — 12, 703/4.
2. = MAP 95,	Bu. 88 — 5 — 12, 210.
3. = CT VIII 29^{a},	Bu. 91 — 5 — 9, 2183.
4. = CT IV 42^{a},	Bu. 91 — 5 — 9, 2188.
5. = CT VIII 12^{c},	Bu. 91 — 5 — 9, 2460.
6. = CT II 40^{b},	Bu. 91 — 5 — 9, 394.
7. = CT VI 37^{a},	Bu. 91 — 5 — 9, 707.
8. = CT II 33,	Bu. 91 — 5 — 9, 366.
9. = CT II 31,	Bu. 91 — 5 — 9, 360.
10. = CT II 41,	Bu. 91 — 5 — 9, 410.
11. = CT VIII 43^{b},	Bu. 91 — 5 — 9, 2465.
12. = CT VI 37^{b},	Bu. 91 — 5 — 9, 709.
13. = CT VIII 34^{b},	Bu. 91 — 5 — 9, 2504.
14. = R 101,	(Kh^{2}) 1524.
15. = CT VI 22^{b},	Bu. 91 — 5 — 9, 365.
16. = CT II 4,	Bu. 88 — 5 — 12, 60.
17. = CT VI 42^{b},	Bu. 91 — 5 — 9, 2470.
18. = MAP 106,	VAT 762.
19. = MAP 110,	VAT 842/843.
20. = CT VI 42^{a},	Bu. 91 — 5 — 9, 2177 A.
21. = CT VIII 45^{b},	Bu. 91 — 5 — 9, 2190.
22. = CT IV 47^{a},	Bu. 88 — 5 — 12, 711.
23. = CT VIII 12^{b},	Bu. 88 — 5 — 12, 160.
24. = CT IV 37^{d},	Bu. 88 — 5 — 12, 626.
25. = CT IV 33,	Bu. 88 — 5 — 12, 580.
26. = CT IV 25^{b},	Bu. 91 — 5 — 9, 712.
27. = R 37,	(J. S.) 27.
28. = CT VIII 22^{b},	Bu. 91 — 5 — 9, 374.

29. = CT VIII 1^{b}, Bu. 91 — 5 — 9, 448.
30. = CT IV 31^{a}, Bu. 88 — 5 — 12, 532.
31. = MAP 70, VAT 766.
32. = CT VIII 15^{c}, Bu. 91 — 5 — 9, 1016.
33. = CT VI 35^{a}, Bu. 91 — 5 — 9, 688.
34. = CT VIII 11^{b}, Bu. 91 — 5 — 9, 503.
35. = CT IV 14^{a}, Bu. 88 — 5 — 12, 216.
36. = CT IV 46^{c}, Bu. 88 — 5 — 12, 655.
37. = CT VI 44^{b}, Bu. 91 — 5 — 9, 2421.
38. = CT VI 40^{c}, Bu. 91 — 5 — 9, 2524.
39. = CT VIII 42^{b}, Bu. 91 — 5 — 9, 2455.
40. = CT VIII 11^{c}, Bu. 91 — 5 — 9, 596.
41. = CT VIII 37^{b}, Bu. 91 — 5 — 9, 1058.
42. = R 85, (Kh^{2}) 1292.
43. = R 25, (J. S.) 78.

In the Semitic part of the glossary I have given the radicals, even when the root of a word does not occur elsewhere, in order to facilitate the identification of the words. The Sumerian words and phrases are given separately, for I am convinced that the clauses written in Sumerian were also read as Sumerian and not as Semitic. This is indicated by "phonetic" [1]) writings which occasionally occur.

1) RU (sign no. 15) instead of RÚ (sign no. 37) in 29, 12; NU.UM-MAL.MAL.A (27, 13) instead of NU-MAL.MAL.A, and even NU.UM-MAL.MAL.JA (CT II 14, l. 15), spoken nummamajja; in the same text (l. 12) we read IB-TA-BAL with IB (sign no. 183) instead of ÍB (sign no. 67); other examples can easily be collected.

Some of the personal names which formerly were read as Semitic I have treated as Sumerian for reasons into which I cannot enter here [1]).

1) Cf. especially the names composed with NANNA(R) and MA.AN-SUM. From the fact that such names were pronounced Sumerian it must not be concluded that the Sumerian language as such was still a living language, or that the bearers of theses names were Sumerians.

May 1907. A. UNGNAD.

1.

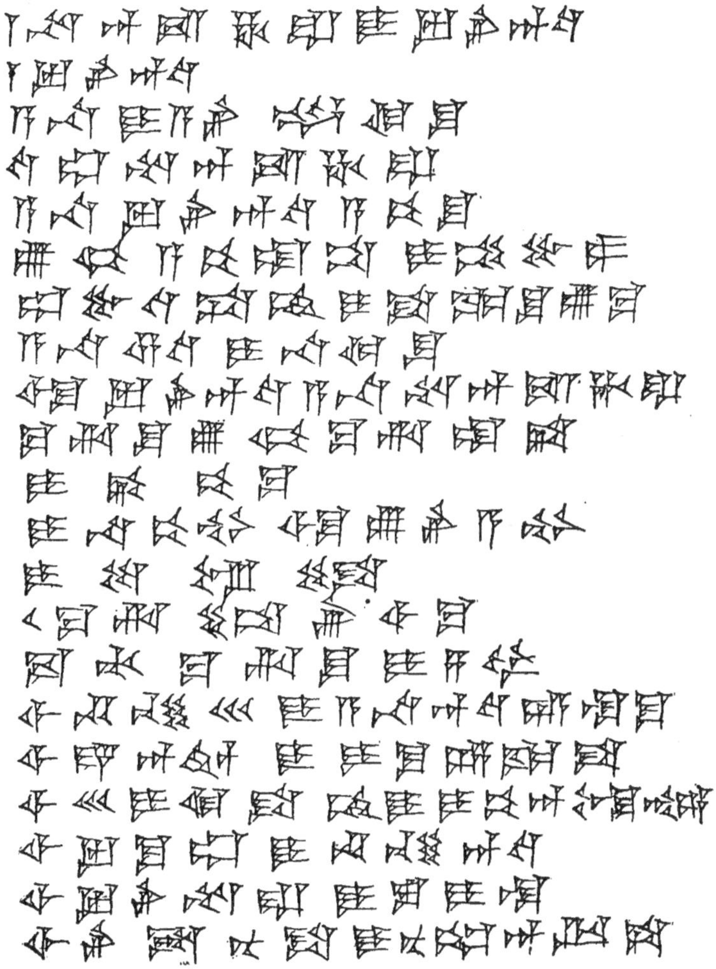

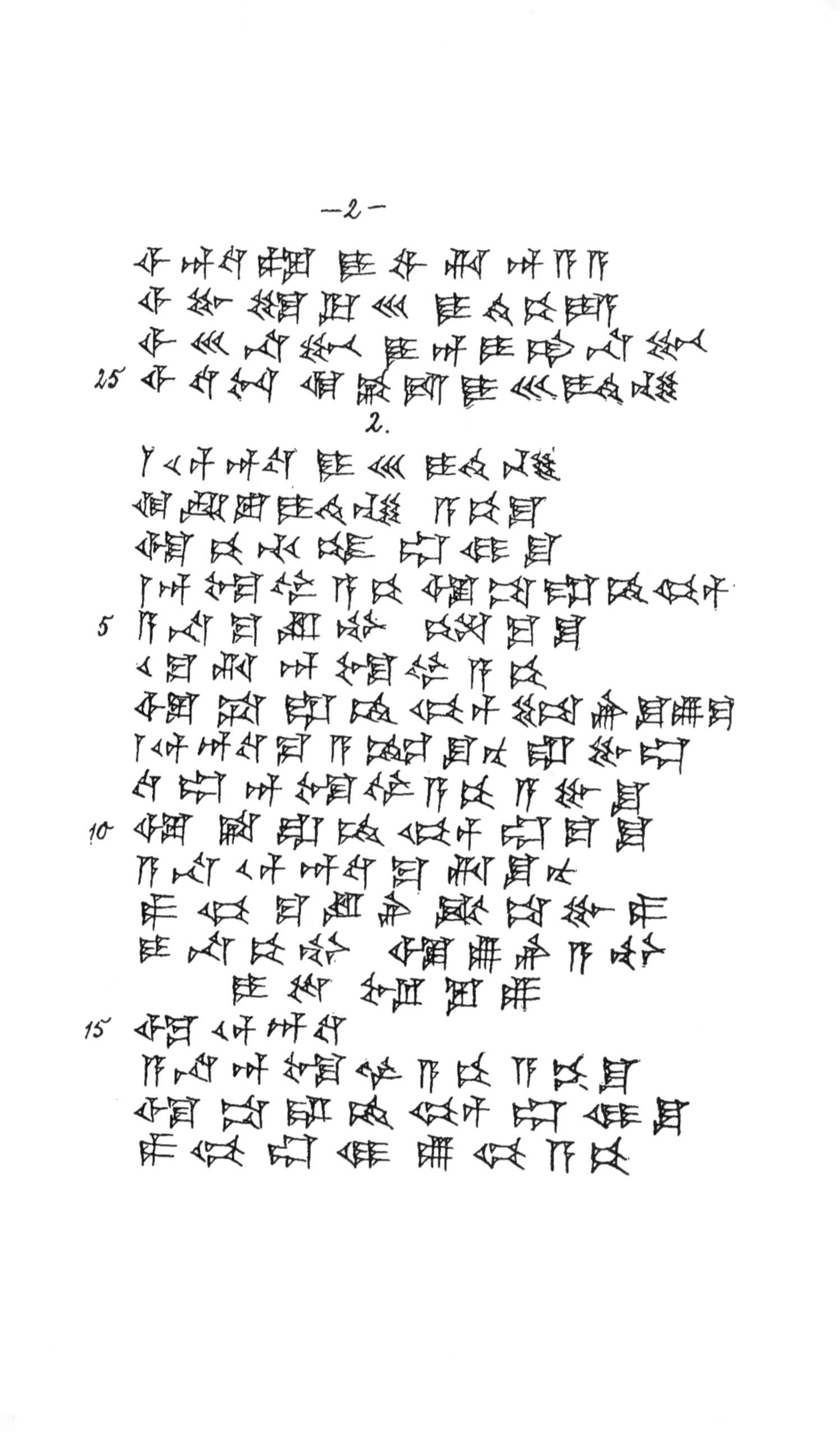

2.

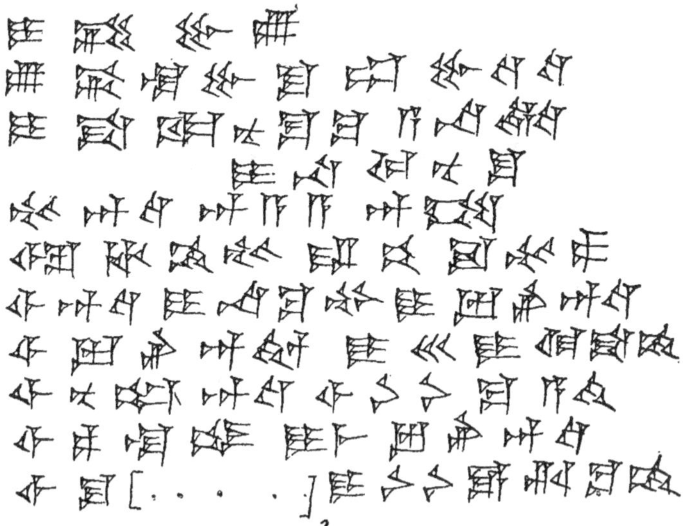

3.

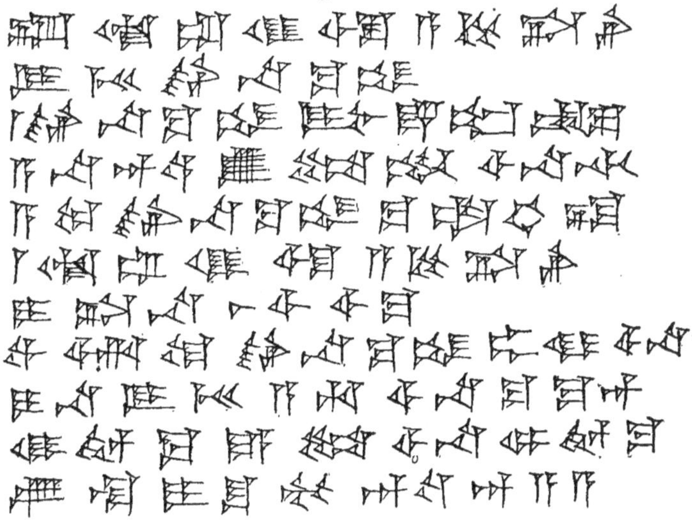

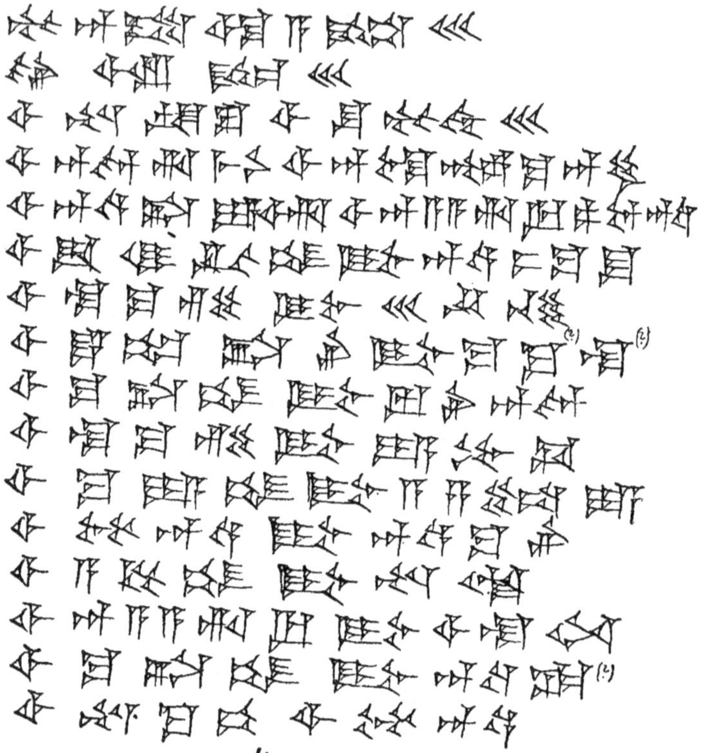

4.

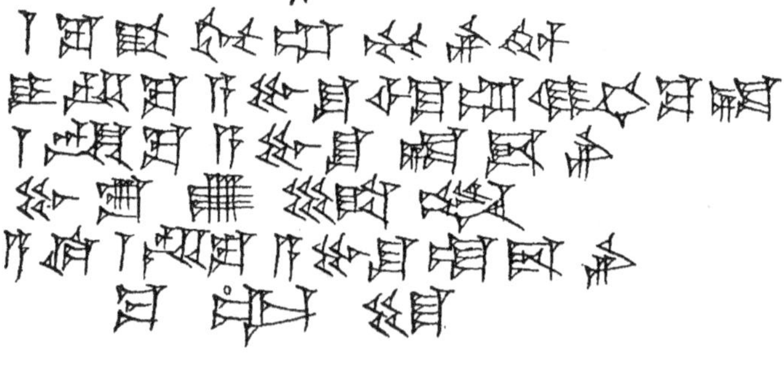

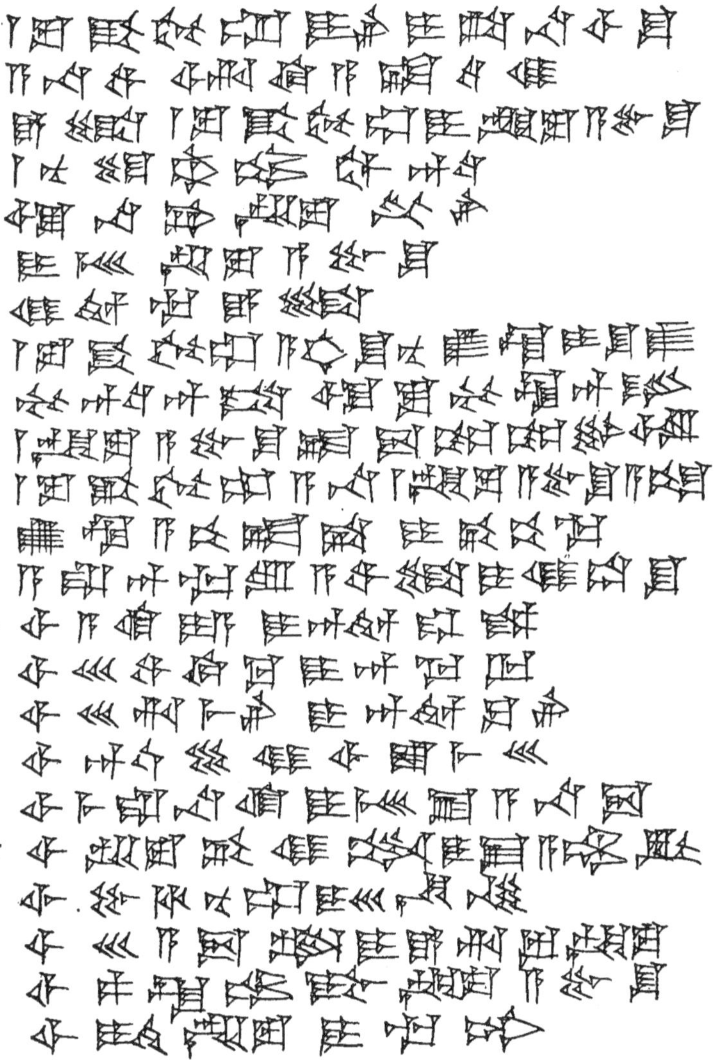

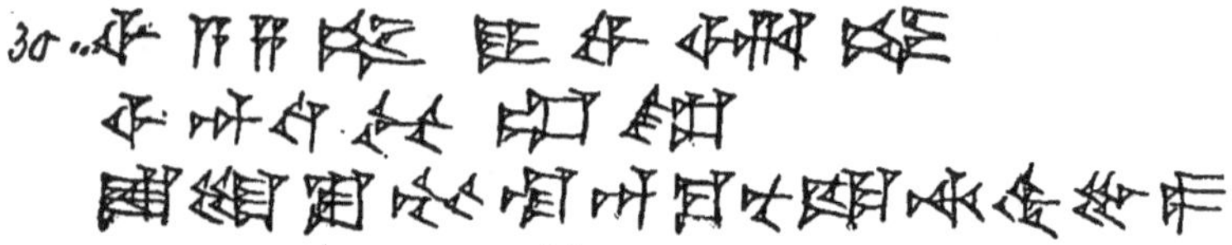

5.

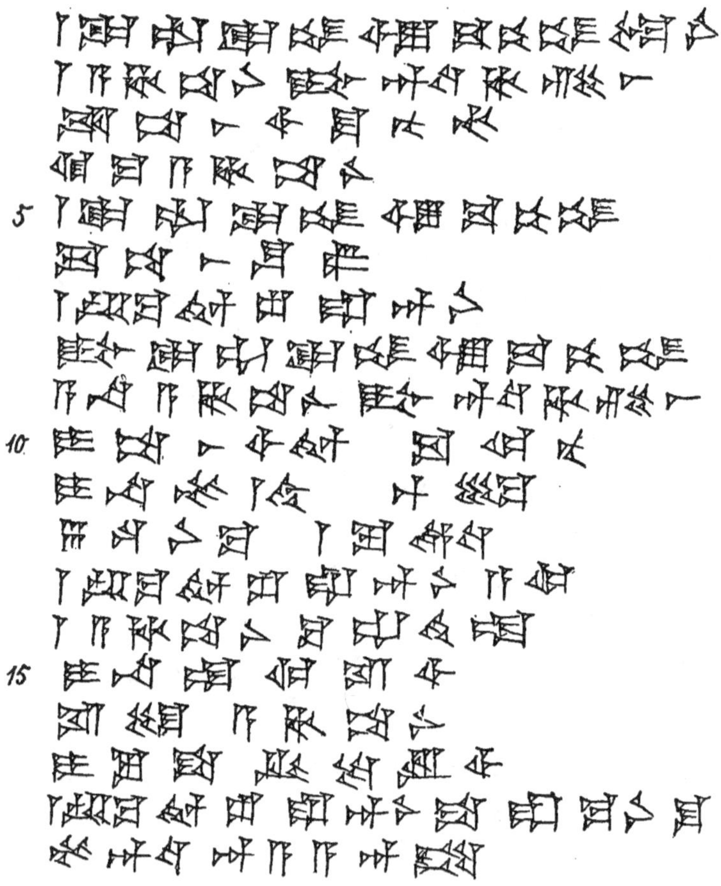

6.

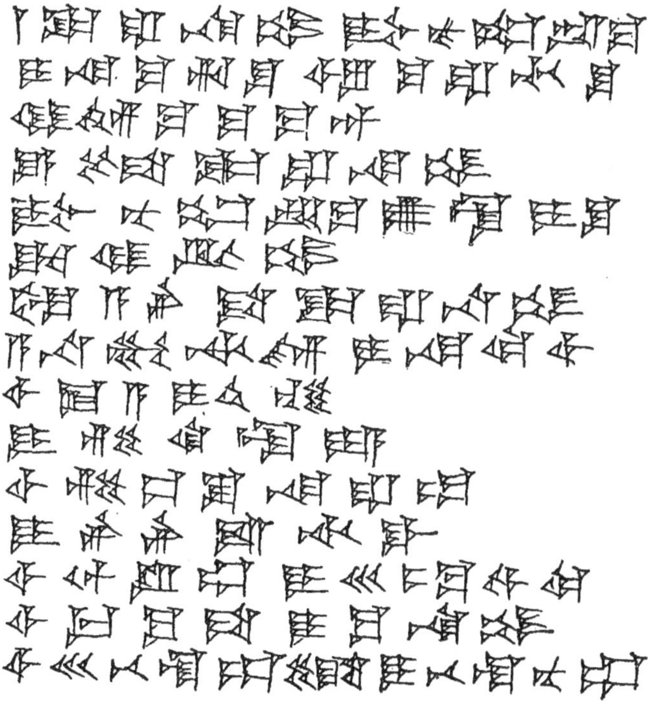

7.

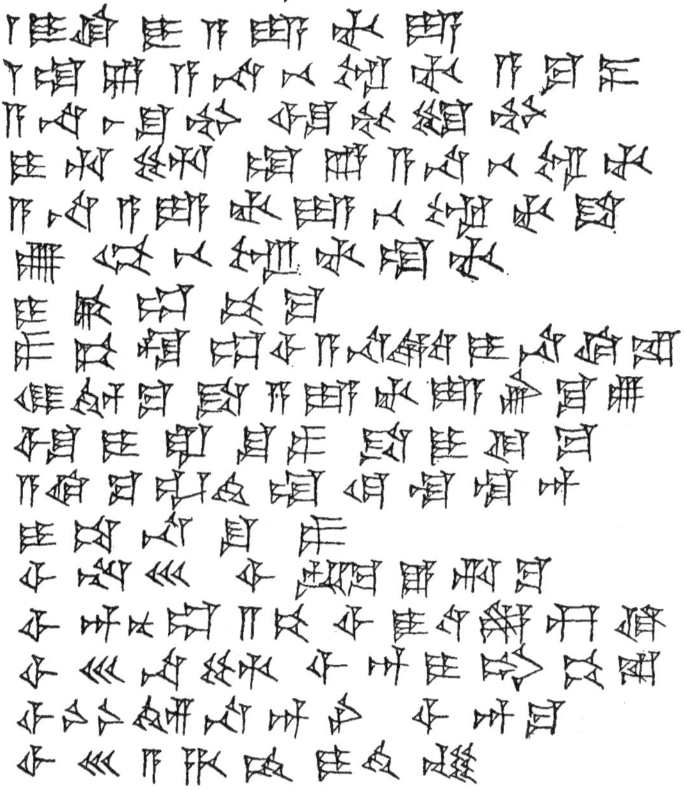

8.

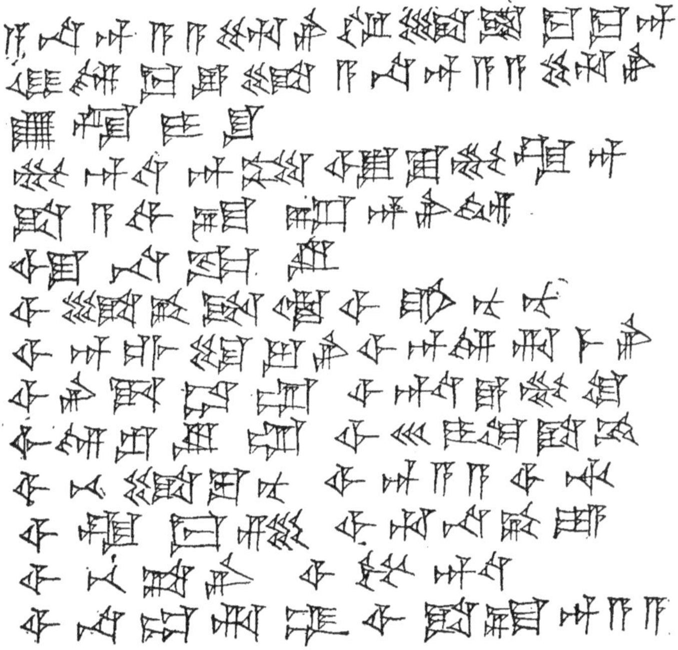

9.

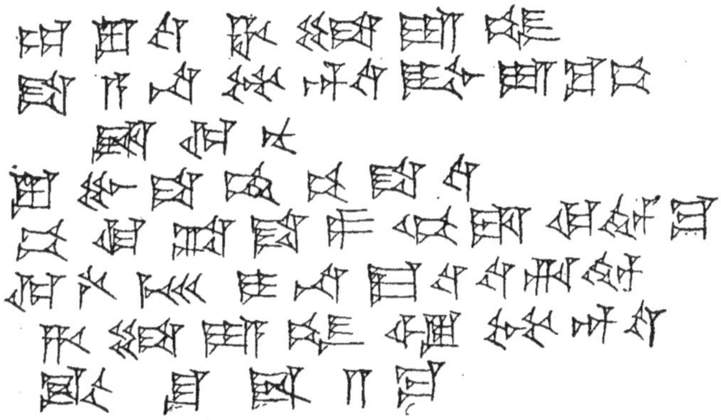

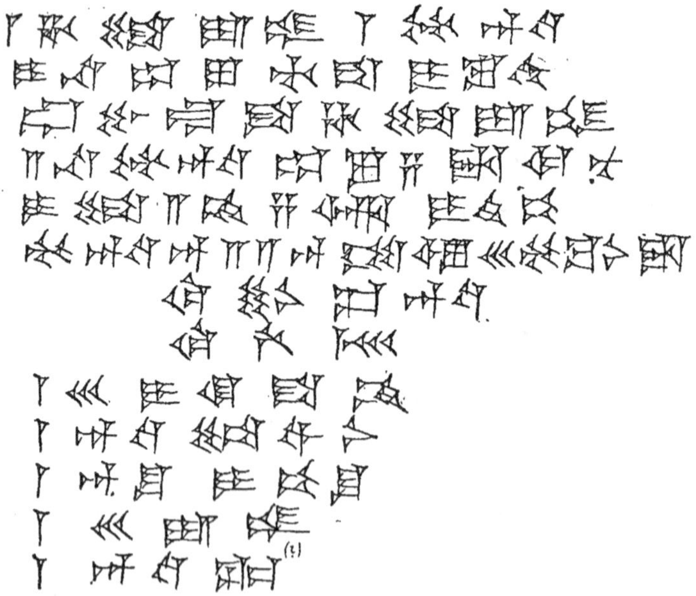

10.

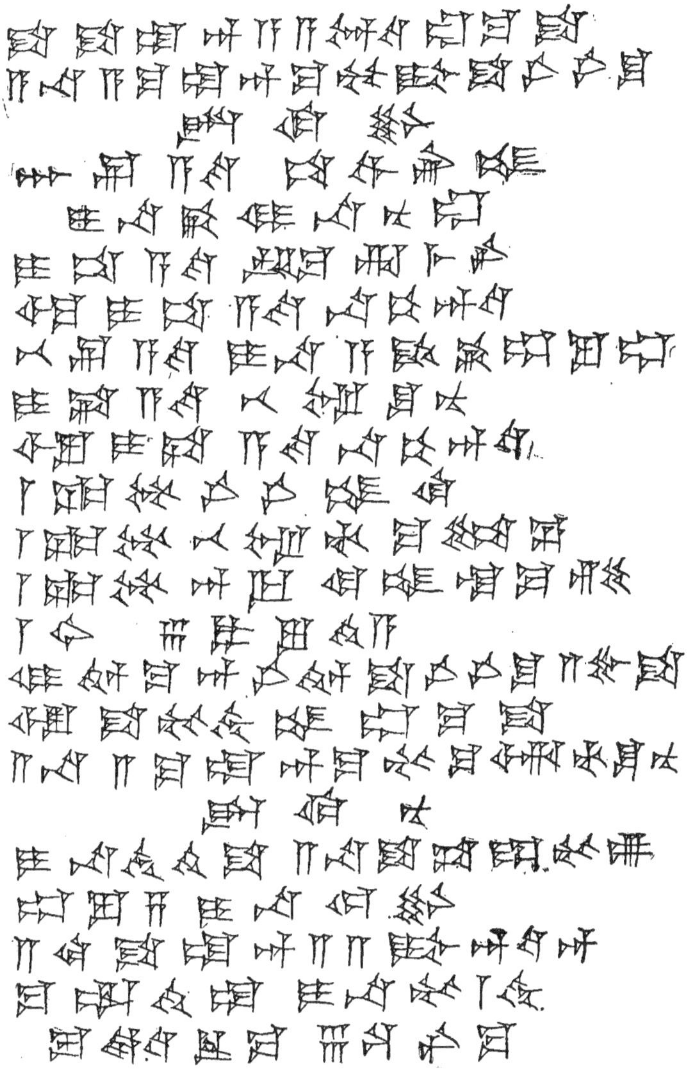

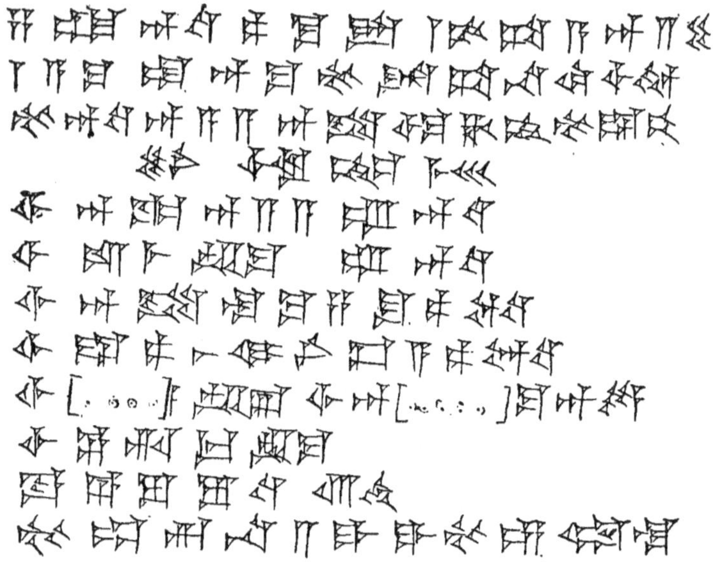

11.

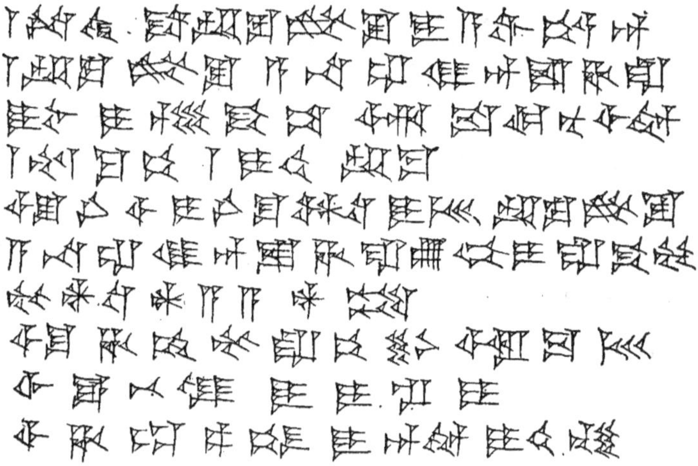

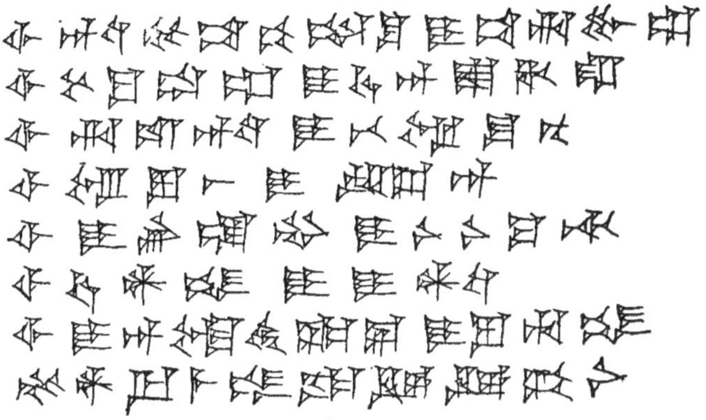

12.

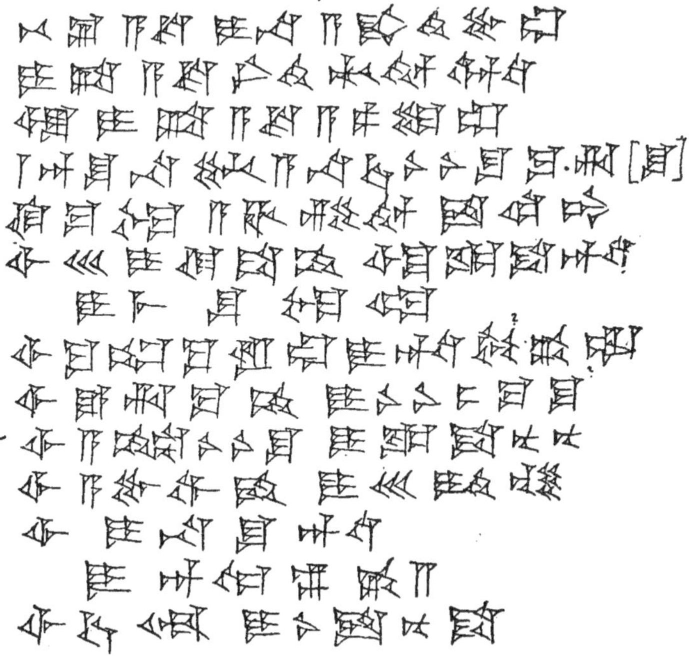

13.

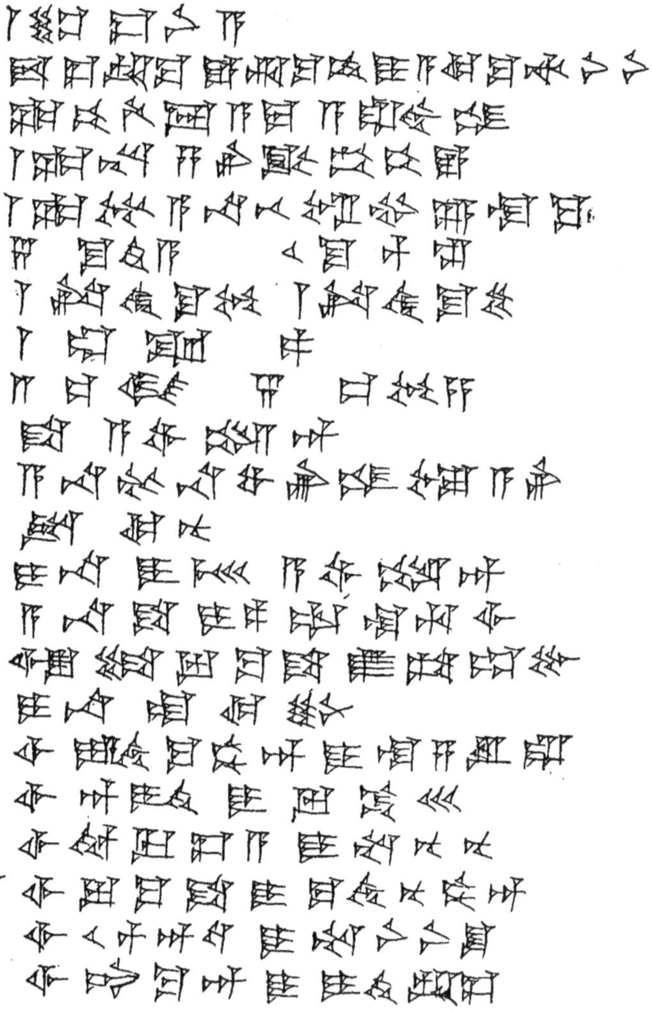

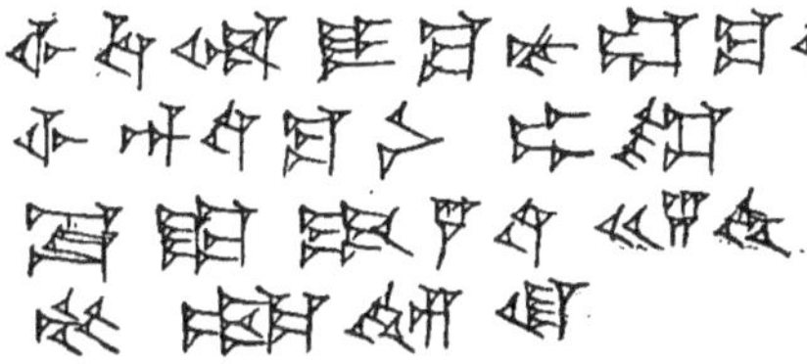

14.

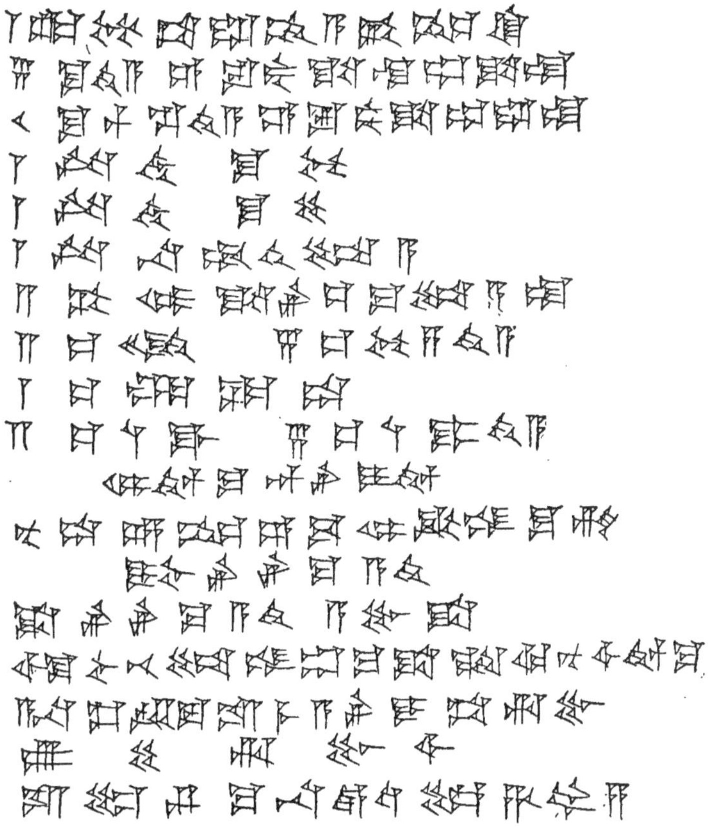

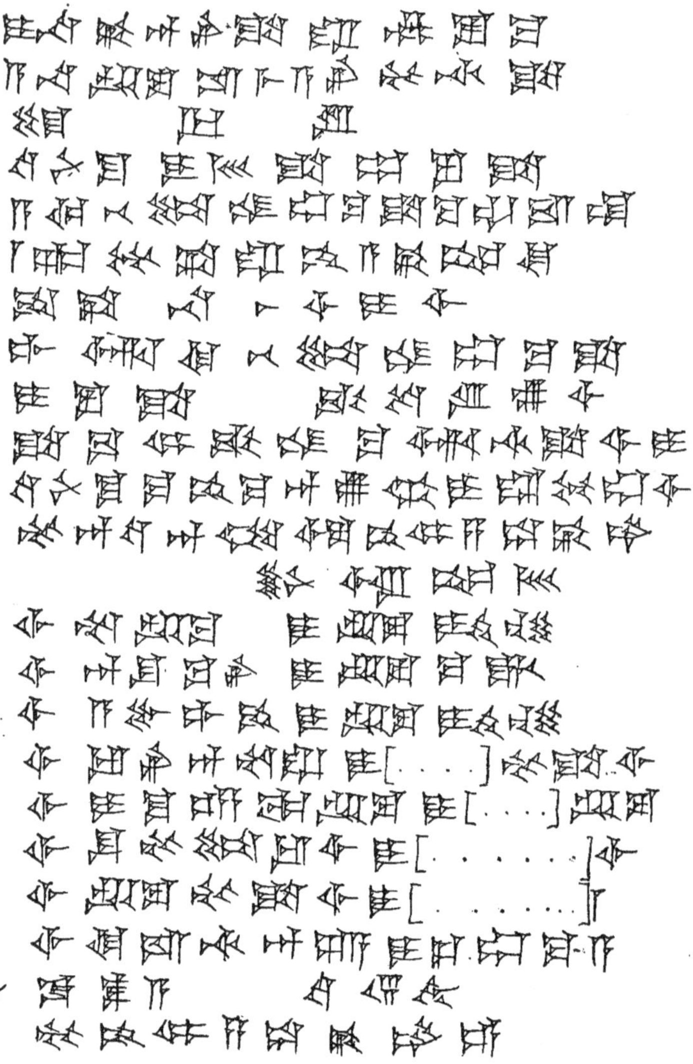

15

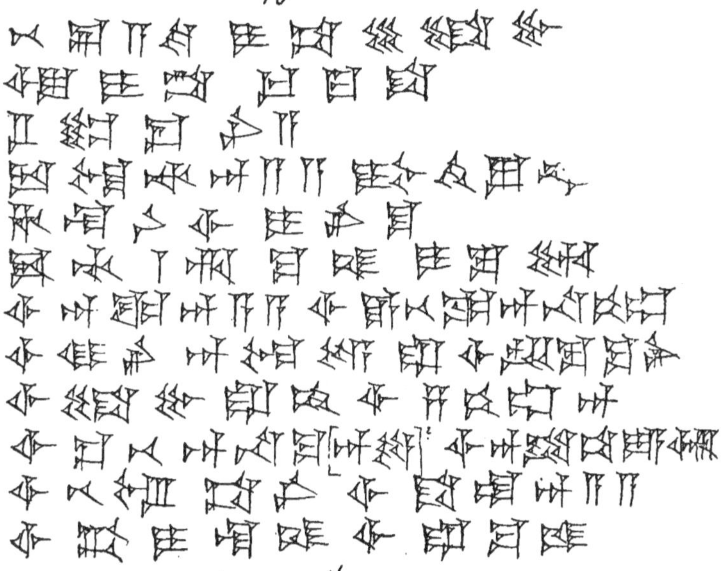

16.

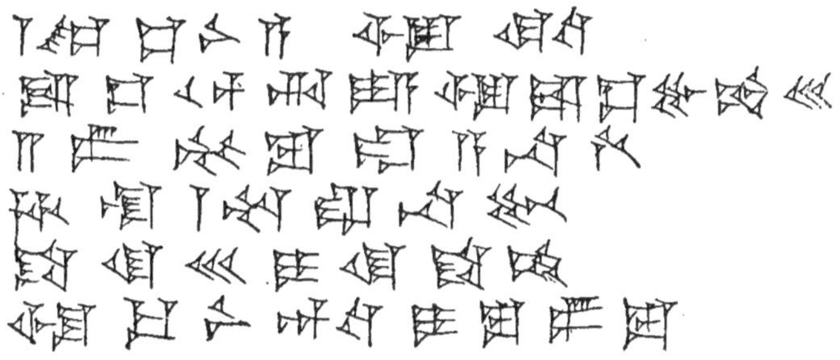

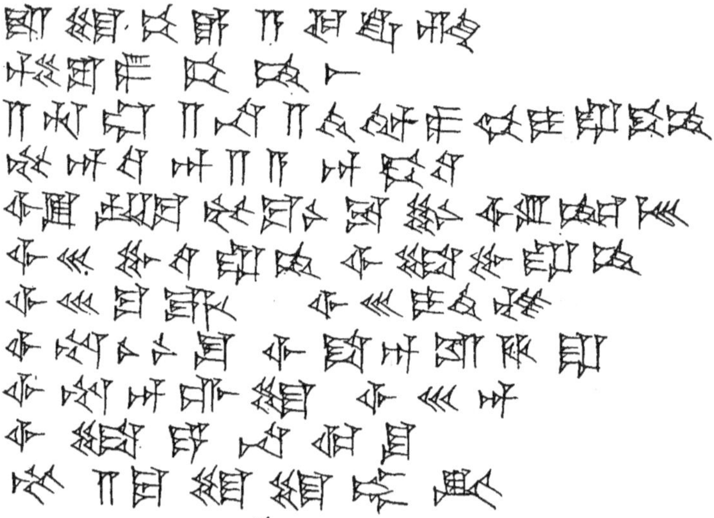

17

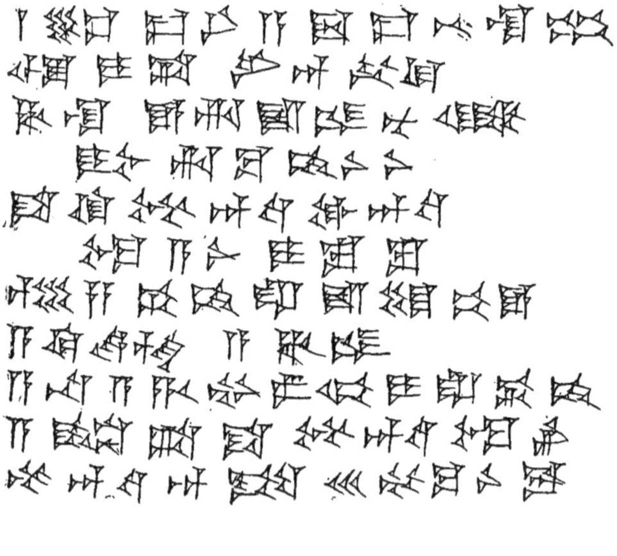

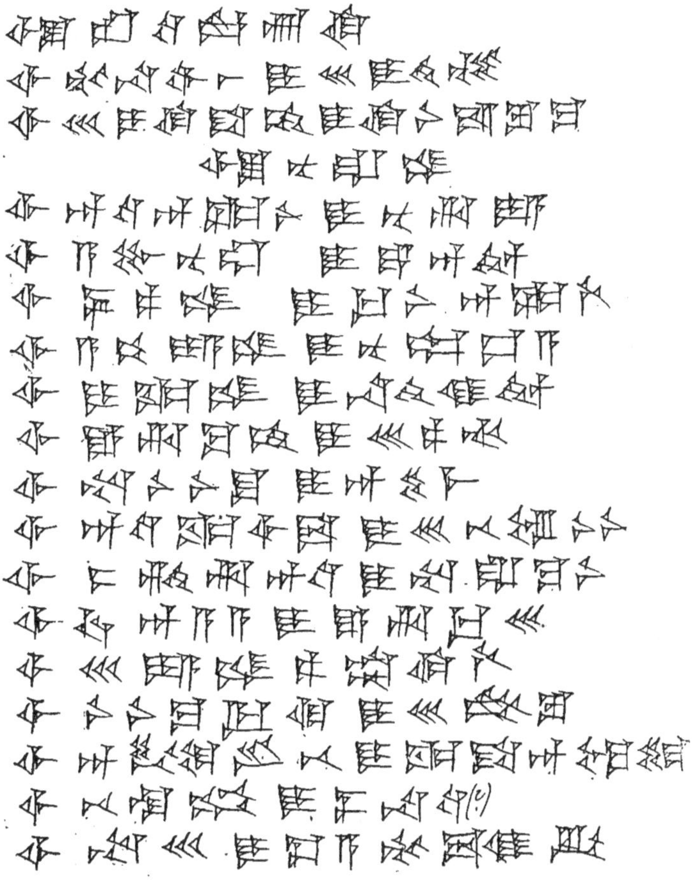

18.

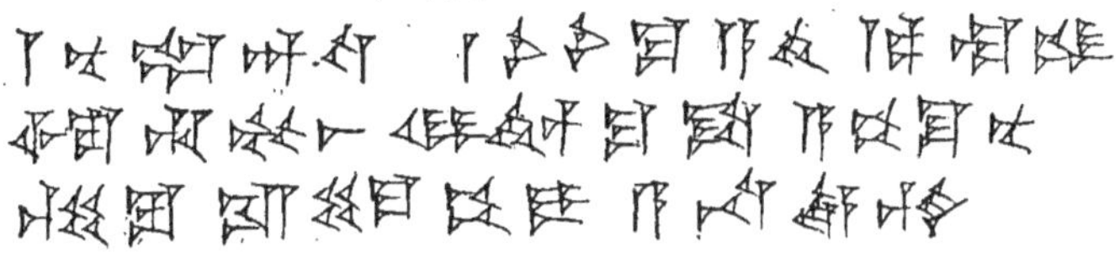

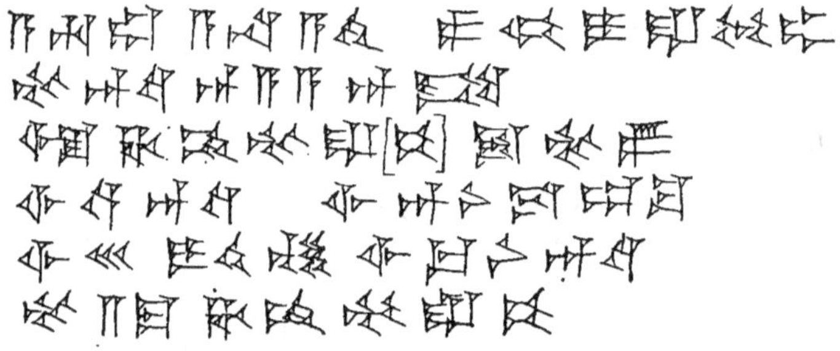

19.

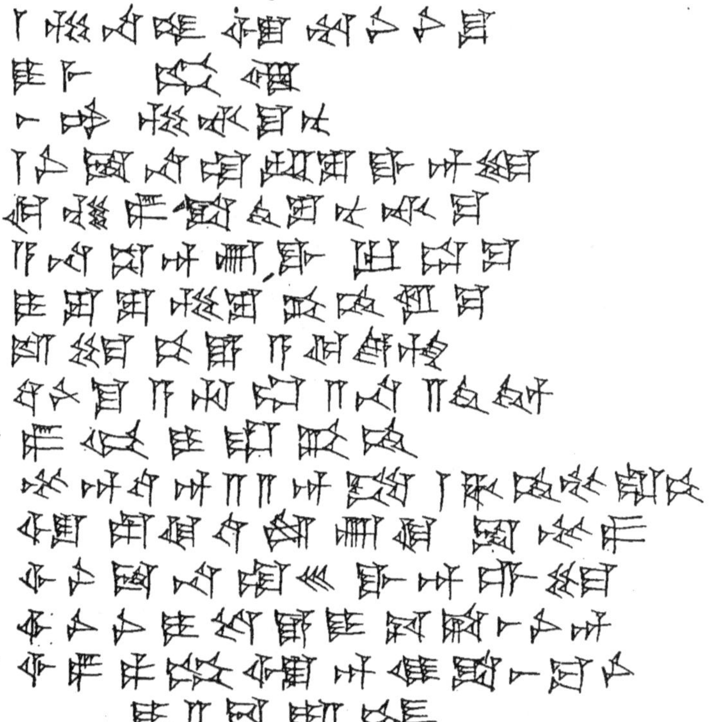

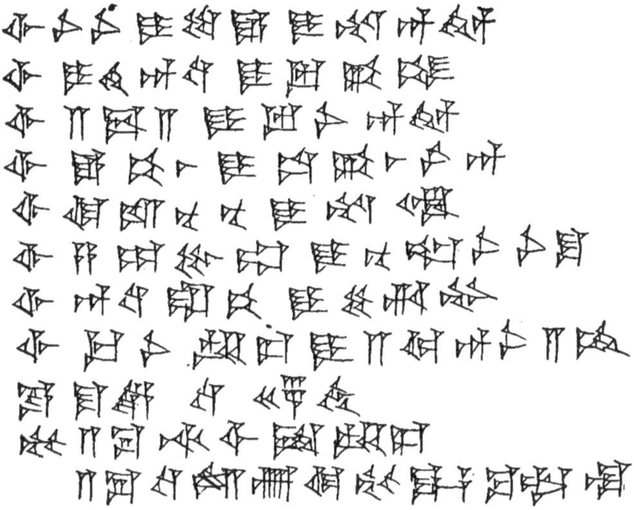

20.

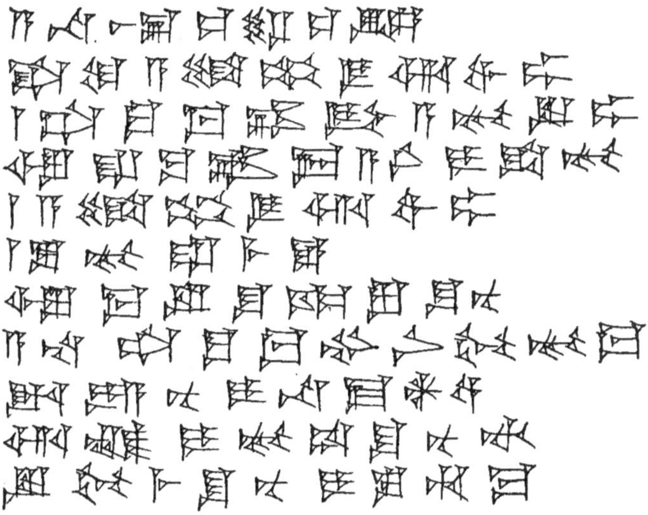

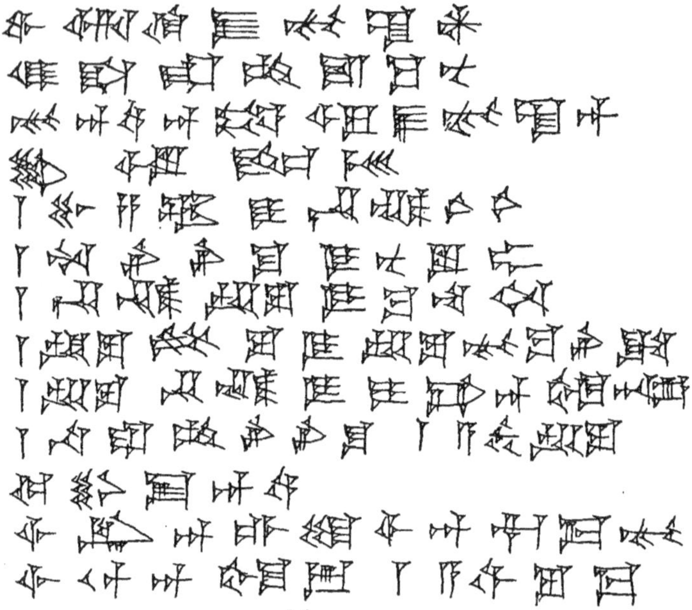

21.

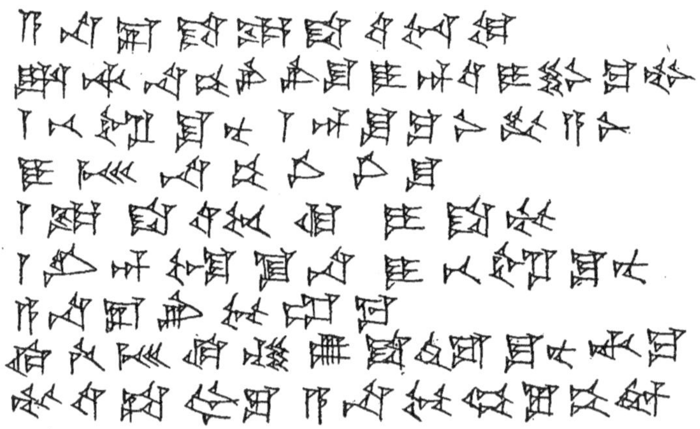

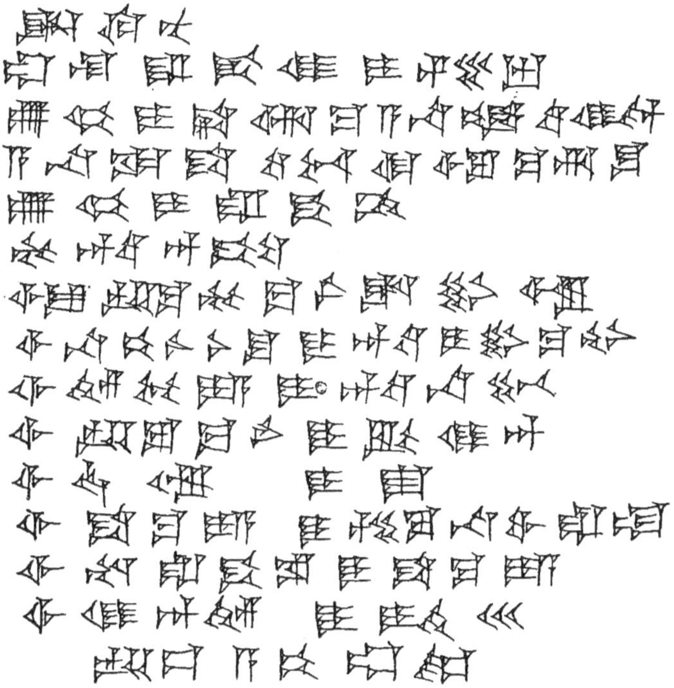

22.

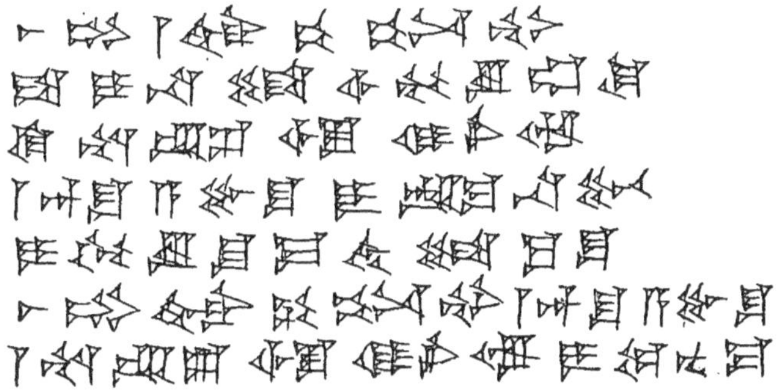

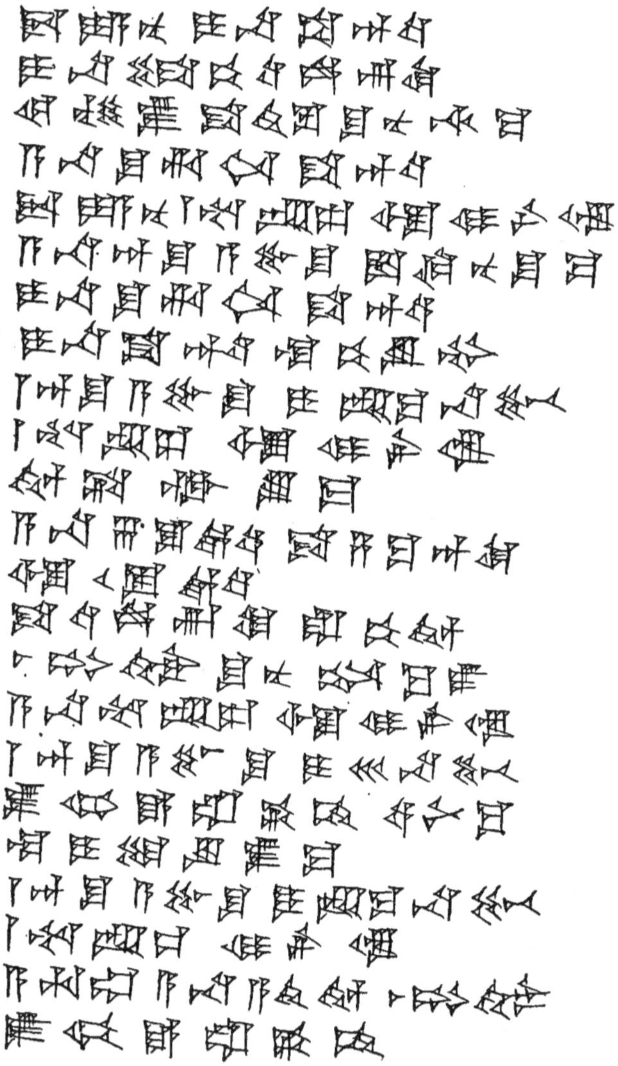

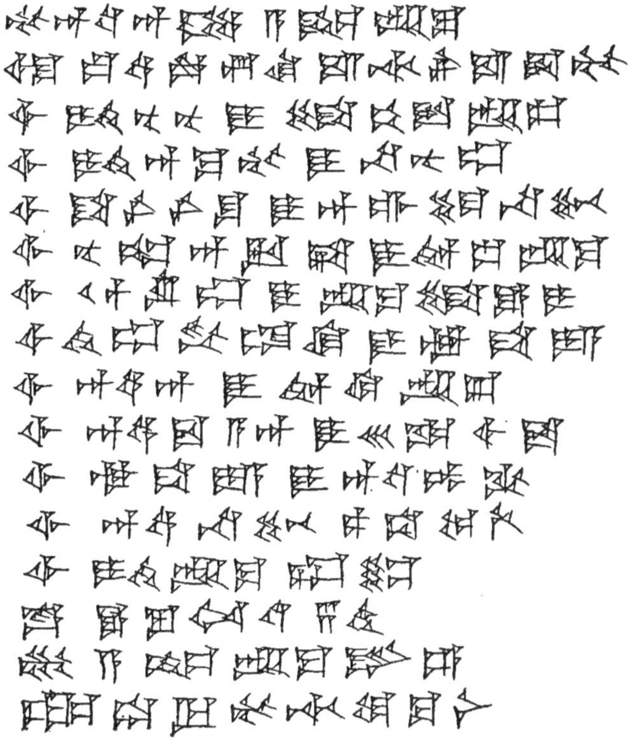

23.

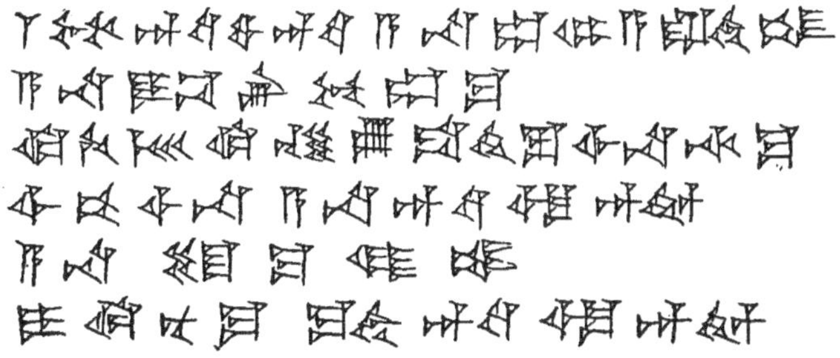

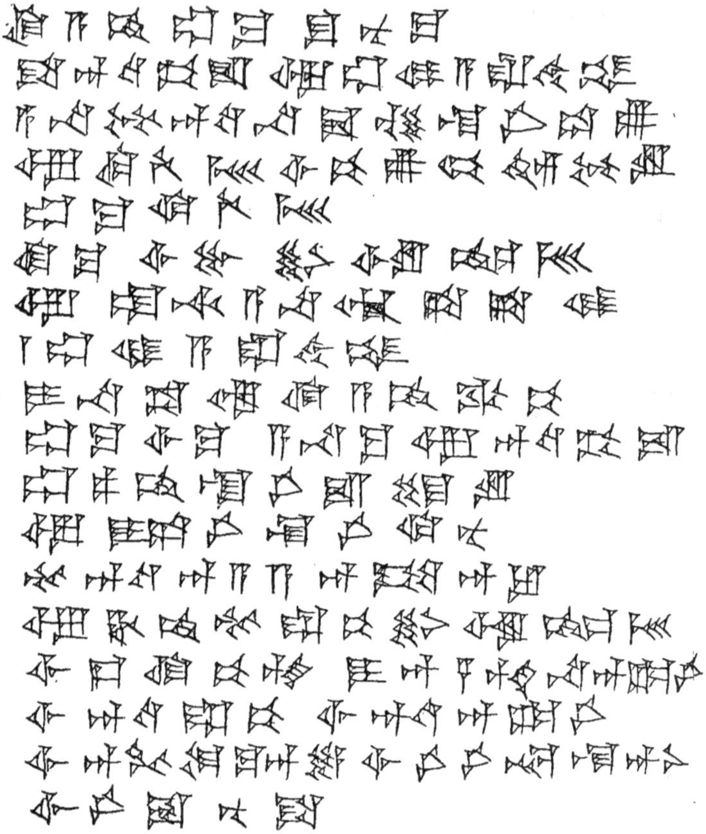

24.

25

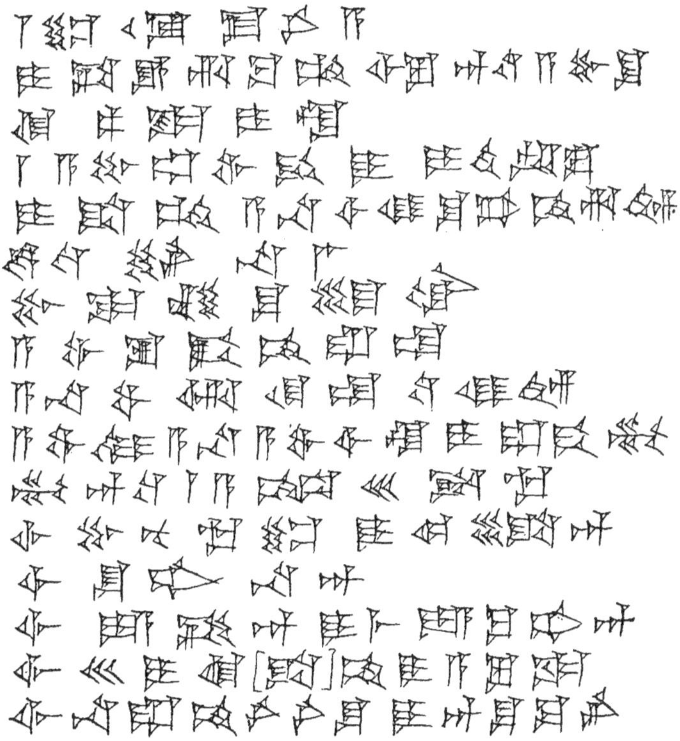

26.

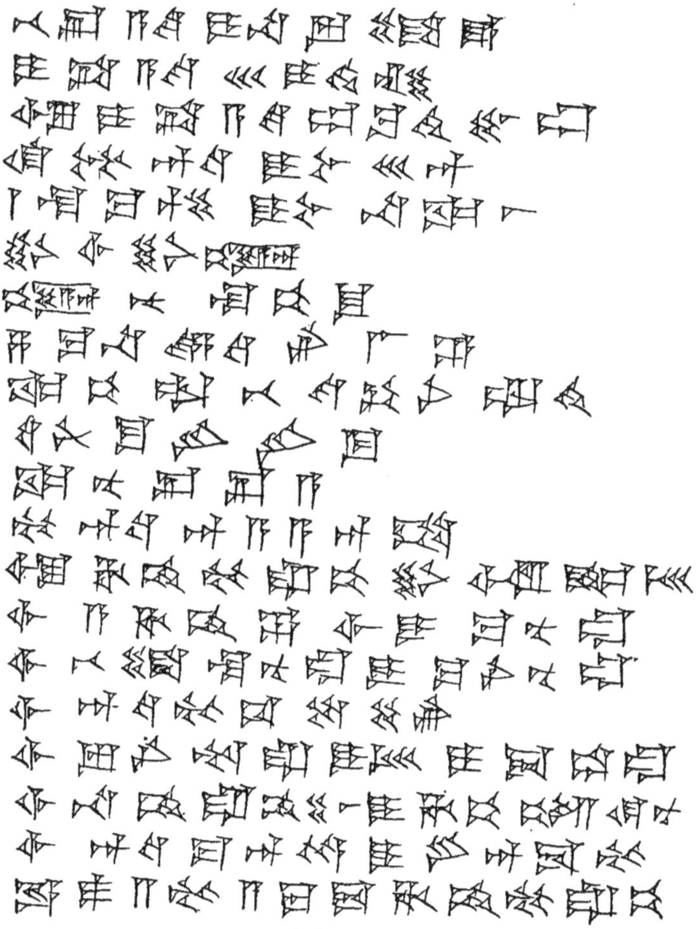

27.

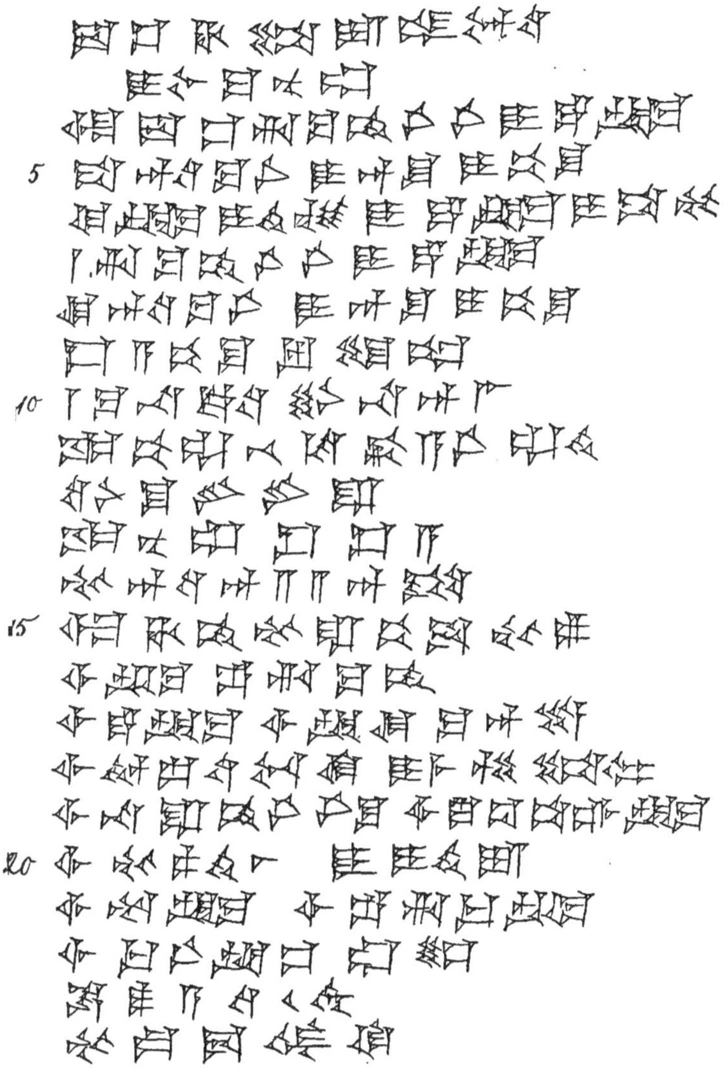

28.

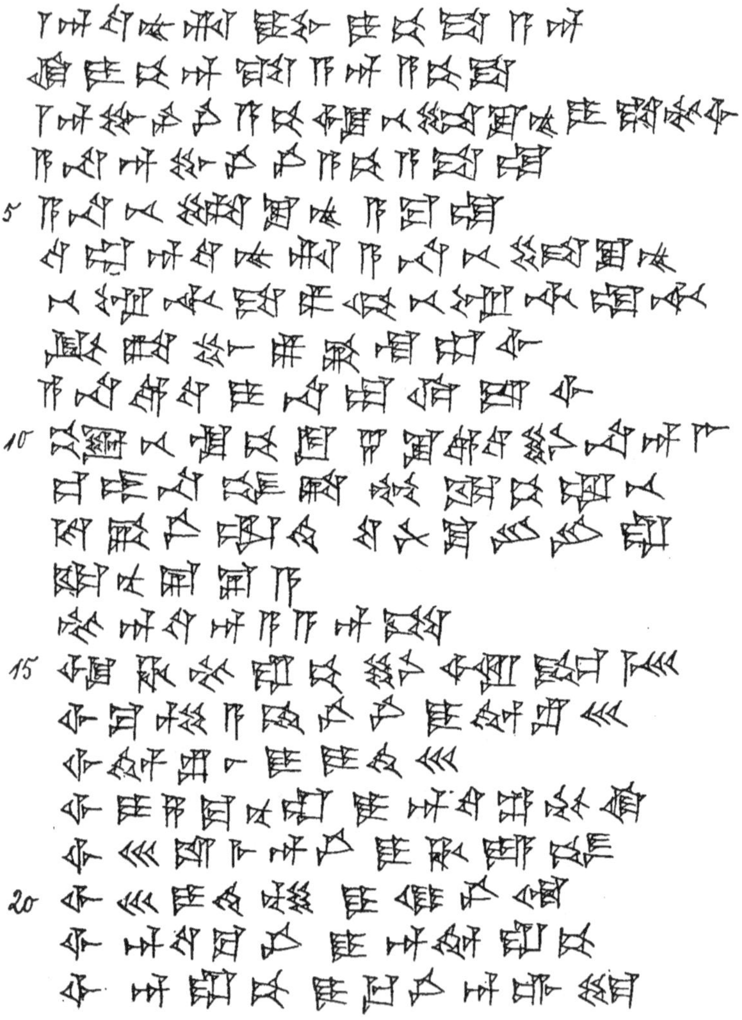

29.

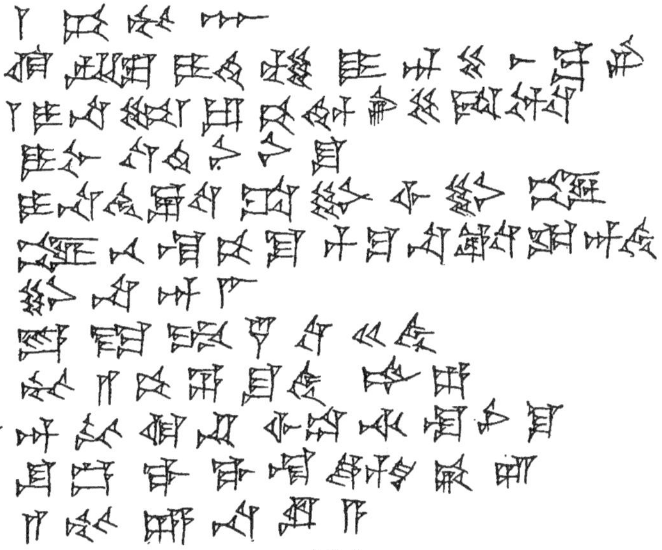

30.

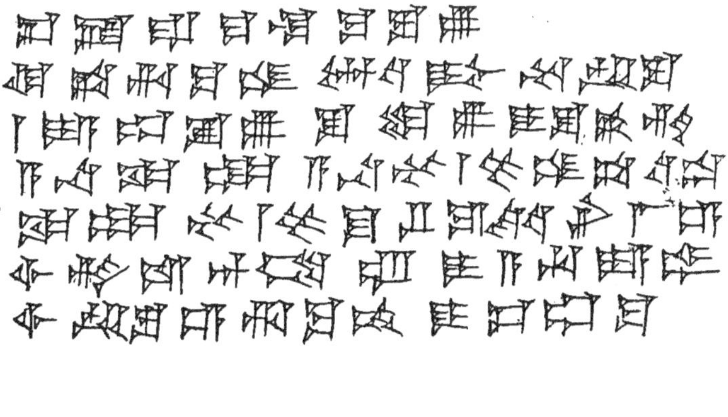

31.

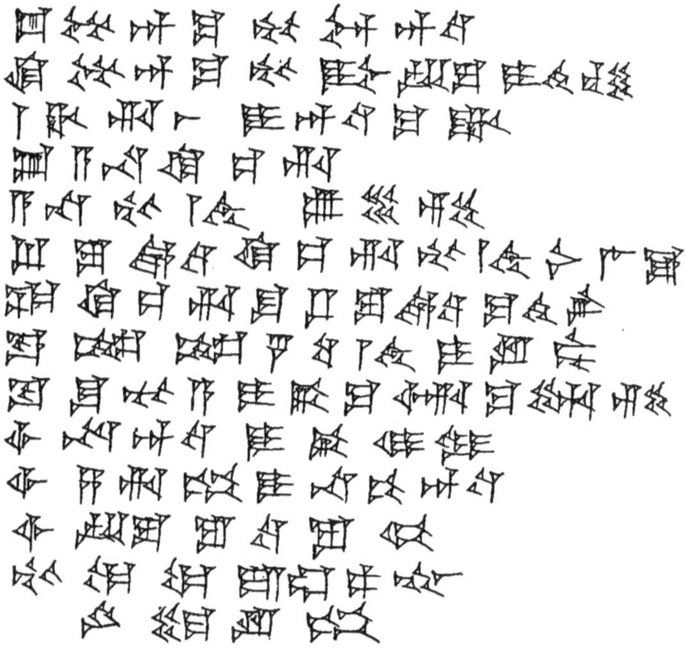

32.

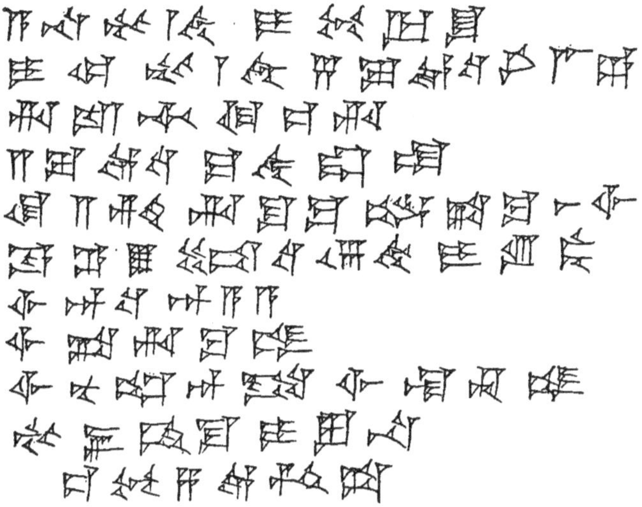

33.

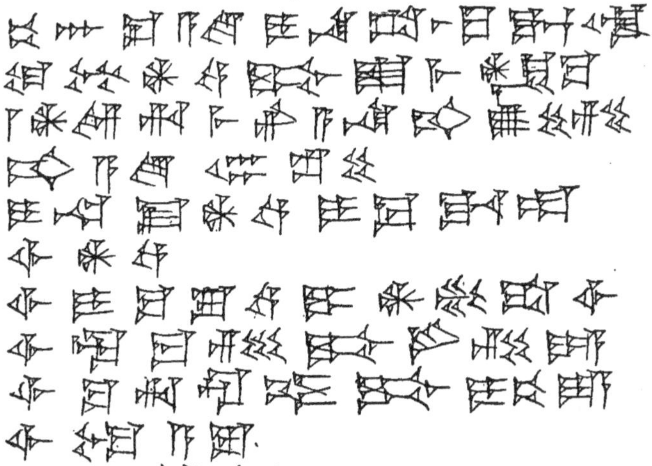

34.

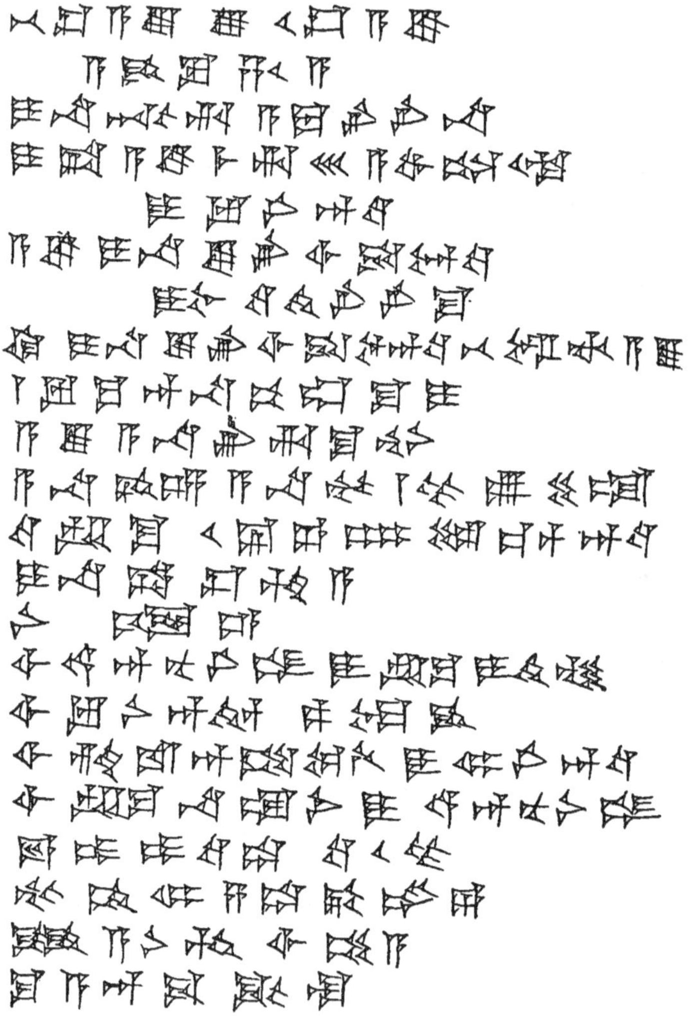

35.

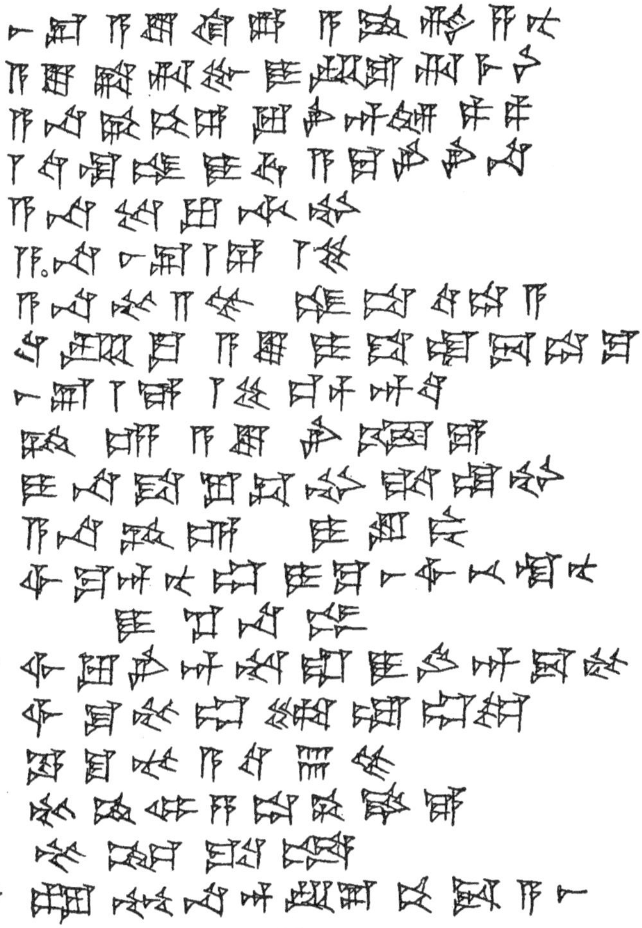

36.

— 36 —

37

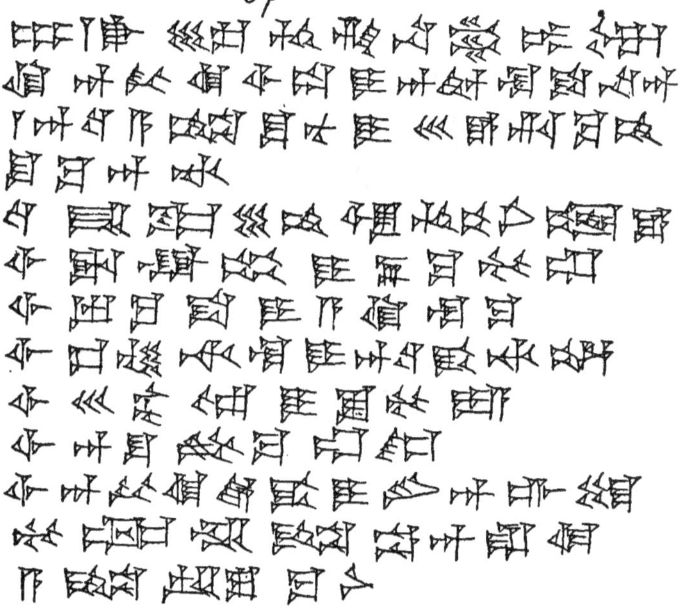

38.

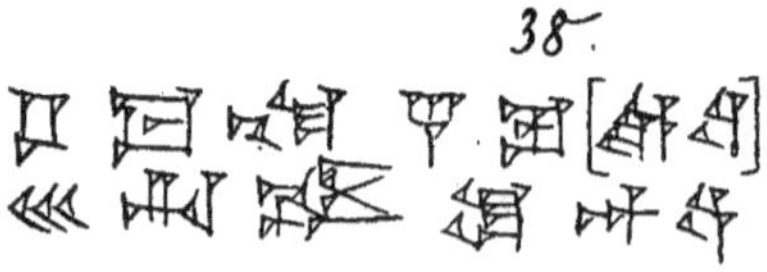

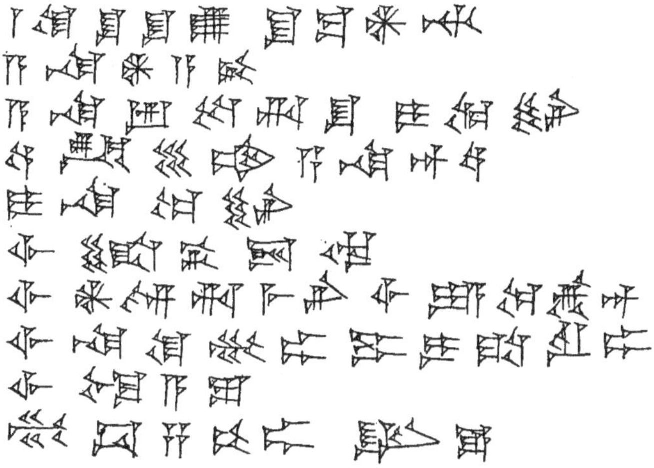

39.

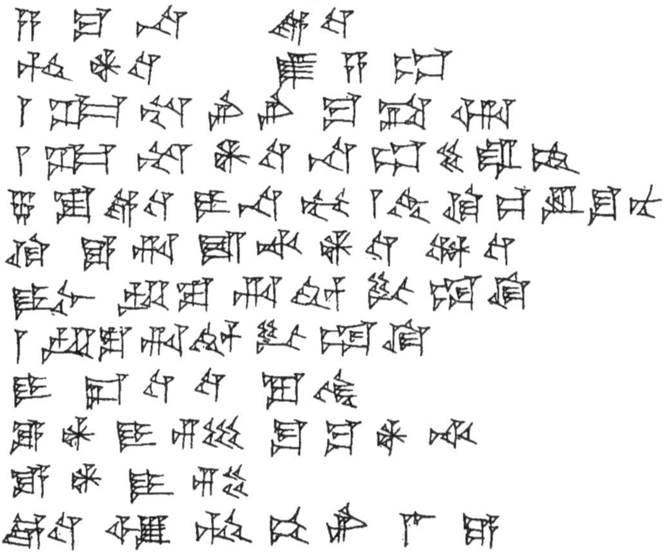

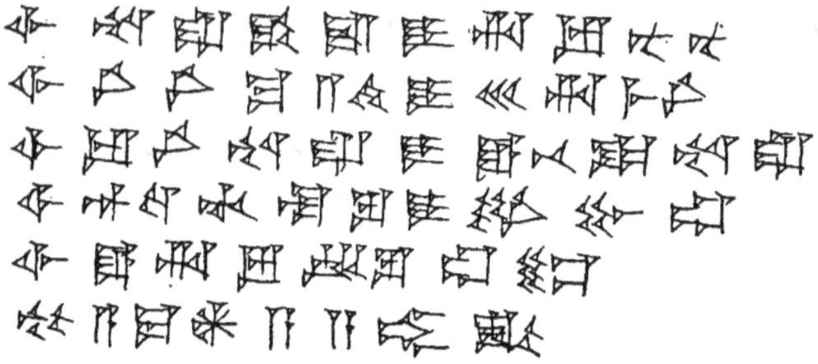

40.

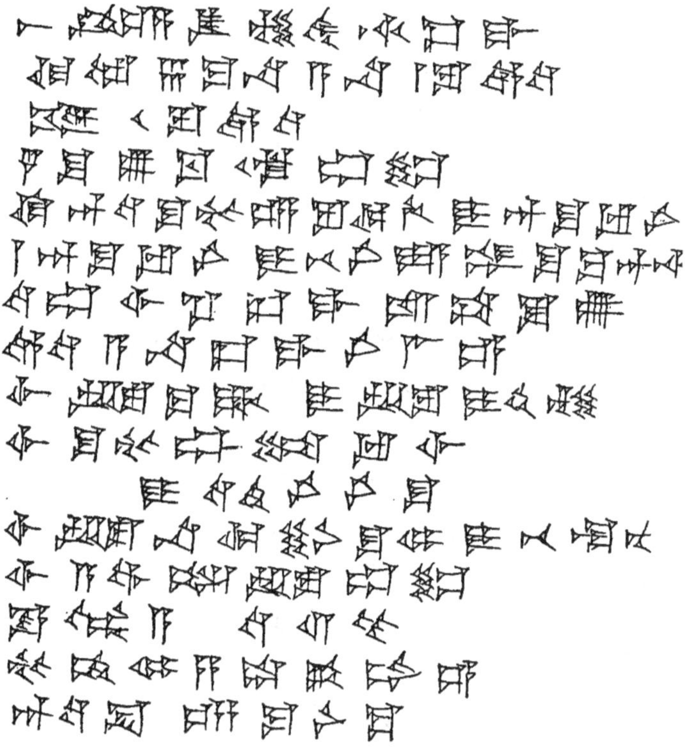

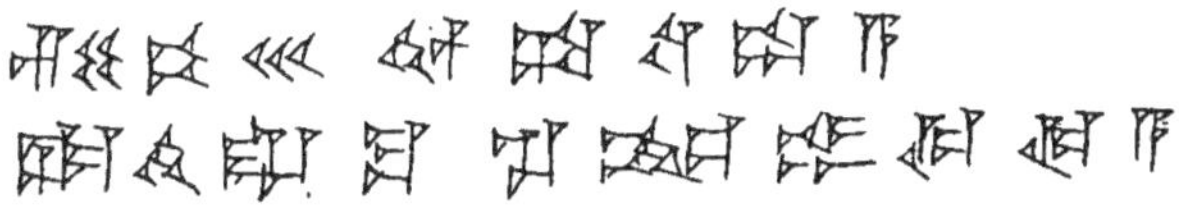

41.

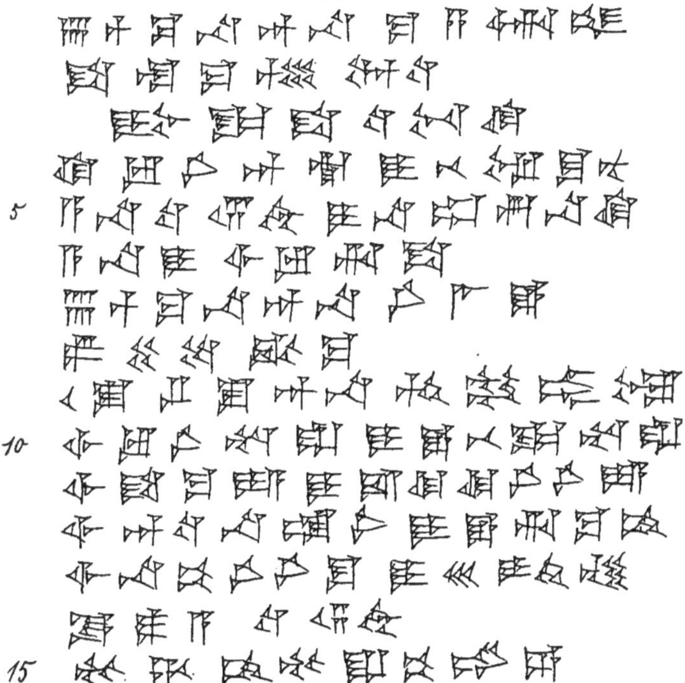

42.

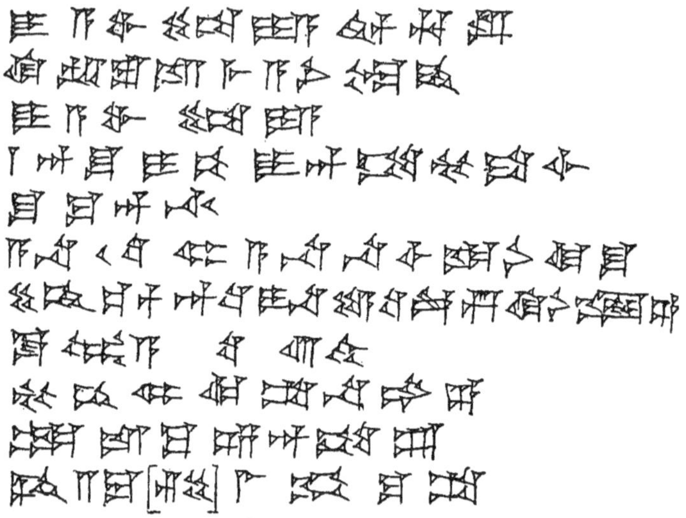

43.

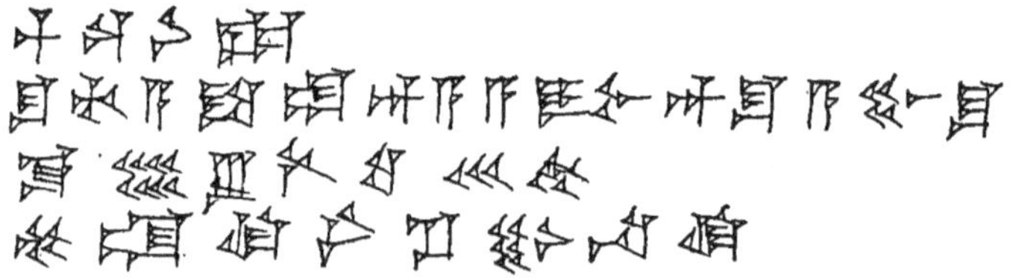

List of signs.

1	aš, ru(m); 1/18(GAN)		Šamaš, UTU
2	a) ḫal; 3) = 6		Rammân
3	šalâšu; 3/18(GAN)		Uraš
4	BAL(=šûtuqu)		Aa
	ebirtu		Sin
5	ŠAḪ		Enlil(Bêl)
6	an, el, ilu, Anu		EN.KI(=Ea)
	} NANNA(R)	7	ag
		8	MAḪ(=ṣîru)
	UR.RA	9	la
	anaku	10	be, tel, 1/3(GAN)
	Annunitum		gmr, gamru
	Rîbu(?)	11	gim
	NINNI(=Ištar)		= 19
	Antum	12	QA (a measure)
	Marduk	13	ši, liqû
	ṣulûlu		balâṭu
	SAK.KUD(=NIN.IB)	14	ig, GAL
	Ea	15	ru
	Amurru		= 4
	DUMU.ZI	16	šir

17 tim
18 UR, wardu
19 mu, šattu, šumu, niš
20 aḫu; cf 6
Uru
21 , , na
= 6
22 , nu
gadištu
23 α) bar, MAŠ, mišlu, 10 QA
= 110, = 9 β) = 6
24 MAŠ (= ṣiptu)
25 ḫu
26 , nam
27 , en
28 ri, tal
birîtu
29 zi, ṣi
30 , gi
kênu
31 nun
α) = + ; β) = 35
32 GAN (a measure)

33 , = 55
= 60
34 , si
35 , , ebûru
36 KUR; cf. 37
37 , α) RU; β) = 38, 40
38 ni, i, li; -šū, -šā
( ) šamnu
piššatu
39 abnu
Semitic values not known
" "
" "
"
aban elît urṣi
40 , , ir
41 , , awilu, MULU
= 153
42 tab (cf. 82); tappû
43 , ḪE
ḫegallu
44 alu;
= 48 54

45	šum; cf. 56
46	erû šinnu
47	α) ab; β) 46, 48, 54
	Tupliaš
48	um
49	ad; cf. 50.
	abu
50	Uruk; cf. 20.
51	ṣi, ṣe
52	BAD (= dûru)
53	isinnu
54	tup, tuppu
	tupšarru
55	GU (= kišâdu)
	biltu
56	ṭur; cf. 45
57	LUGAL, šarru
58	du, RA
59	ur
60	il
61	uš, šiddu
62	iš, mil
63	α) bi, pi, -šú, 2/3 (GAN); β) = 92
64	ub
65	qu(m), kum
66	AG (= mdd)
67	tum, dum, ÍB
68	warkâtu
69	ŠAM
	šâmu; šîmu
70	gab; qab
71	DAḪ (= jsp)
72	ta, ṭa
73	bâbu
	Bâbilu
74	ellatu
75	α) KA, pî, ENIM
	awâtu; β) = 76
	kiṣru
76	KA (= SUB, karâbu)
77	warḫu
	Waraḫsamna (8)
	" Kislimu (9)
	" Abu (5)
	" Nisannu (1)
	" Šabâṭu (11)

Du'ûzu (4)
" Tašrîtu (7)
" Simânu (3)
" Addaru (12)
" Elûlu (6)
78 , am
79 šîru
80 α) ne, DE; β) = 81
81 , bil, iššu
82 , , sa
83 pa, ḫat, 20 QA, aklu; an official ⌊cf. 102
84 rê'û, SIB
85 (=) lal
86 α) iṣ; β) = 94, 101
GIŠ.BAR; Semitic value not known
iṣ passûru
iṣ bukânu
iṣ ṣumbu
iṣ eršu
iṣ kirû
iṣ itqurtu
iṣ kussû
iṣ gišimmaru
87 ummu, AMA; cf. 162
88 , al
89 šaggû
90 α) alpu; β) = 91, 92
91 karpat šikkatu
92 , , , ga, qa
93 v. 55
94 , , α) ê, bîtu; β) = 101
rugbu
êkallu
igaru
Ebarbarrum
95 , gurru
96 mar
97 α) šak, SAG, riš, rêšu, reštû, pûtu; β) = 103
(or) wardu (or amtu)
qaggadu
= 72
= 49
α) = 63; β) = 92

98	e; cf. 99, 179
99	ner, nir
100	α) GA, MA(L) β) = 94, 101
	Gagum
101	LIL, GE; cf. 6
102	u, ammatu
103	in … q. v.
104	α) tak, β) kal
	= 67
105	un, KALAM
106	i
107	ja
108	ra
	cf. 117/8; … cf. 62
109	gar
110	ma
	manû
111	α) ba; β) = 113
112	aš, 30 QA
	cf. 35
113	zu, (su); cf. 114
114	GIN (a measure), šiqlu
115	bur
116	gir
117	α) da, ṭa, iṭa; β) = 118
118	α) id; β) cf. 117
119	DUMU, mâru, ṣiḫru
	mârtu
	ablu, ablûtu
	(…) "scribe" (ṭupšarru ?)
	= 14
	= 92
	? (4, 20)
120	ša
	= 80
121	ALAM (= ṣalmu)
122	40 QA
123	šu, qâtu, gimillu
	liqû
	milqîtu
	Sem. value not known
	gallabu
124	gal, qal, rabû
125	su; cf. 114
	α) = 98; β) = 179

	= 105	140	aššatu
126	u, ešerit, 1 (GAN)		ṭamgaru
127	Ištar	141	etc. „priestess of Šamaš" (Sem. val. not known)
128	mi, ṣillu	142	NIN, eriš, aḫâtu, bêltu
129	SUN, GUL	143	gu
129a	littu; = 171	144	amtu
130	ul	145	el
131	nim		= 136
132	ši, lim, IGI, înu, maḫar	146	α) as; β) GIR
133	ar	147	ug
134	PAD (= ṭamû)	148	lum
135	etc. ṣi, û	149	? (27, 24; ŠEG?)
136	di, ṭi, SILIM, SA	150	lam
	dajânu, dînu	151	kur
137	ki, qi, itti; irṣitu, ašru	152	še, še'u
			epru
	nidûtu	153	bu, pu
	maḫîru	154	ṣir
	= 179	155	ṭer
138	eš, Sin	156	li, le
139	sinništu (determ.)	157	us
	ṭupšarratu	158	te, ṭe

159  kar, kâru
160 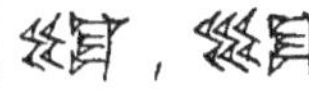 ku, ḳu
161  determ. after numerals
162  KUD ; sûqu
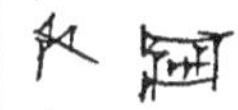 rêbitu
163  ud, tam, bar, pir, ûmu, U
 ana matêma
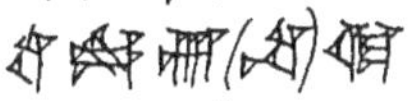 Sippar
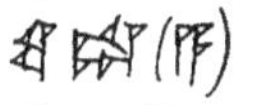 E (= waṣû)
164 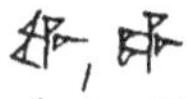 wa, we, wi, pi; ja
165  Kêšu
166  α) = 163 ; β) = 184
167  SUM (= ndn)
168 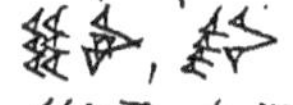 in
169  SAR (a measure)
170 
ŠAG (GA) (= libbu)
171  α) ḫi, ṭa, DUG (= ṭâbu),
ŠAR ; β) = 172
172 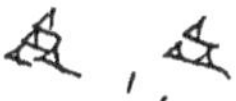 din
173 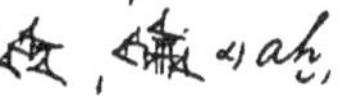 α) aḫ, iḫ, uḫ
β) = 174, 175.

174  kam ; determ. after numerals
175 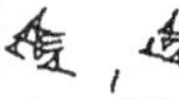 ḫar, mur, šewiru
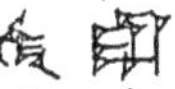 ḫubullu
 šewiru
176 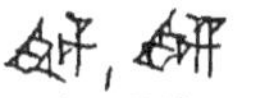 im, MER
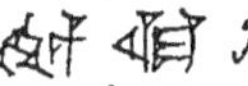 Bît-Karkara
177  imêru
178  sign of collectivity
179  AZAG
 KUBABBAR, kaspu
 GUŠKIN, ḫurâṣu
 = 169
 = 75
180  išten; determ. before personal names; 60GA
181  me ; plural sign
182  MEŠ, plural sign
183 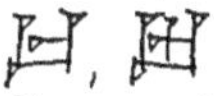 ib
184  ibqu
 etc. v 139 ff.
 = 82
 = 14

185	ku, qu, ŠU; ṣubâtu	195	a) šina, šanû; β) = 196
	parsigu	196	a
	qêmu		-šû, -šâ, cf 38
186	lu, DIB		Akkadû
	= 114		ID(.DA), nâru
	= 119		Purattu
187	šipâtu		ugaru
	lubuštu		eqlu
188	SU	197	1/3 (šuššânu)
189	LA(L) (= šql); la	198	ur, lik, taš
190	tul	199	2/3 (šinipu)
191	ṣar	200	za, ṣa
	= 170	201	ḫa
192	ŠAG		zittu
193	KAB	202	GAR; 12 ammatu
	= 201		bušû
194	ṣênu		kittu

Measures etc.

… (= 1 gurru) = 5 … = 30 … = 300 …

… (= 1 GAN) = 1800 SAR

… (= 1 biltu) = 60 manê = 3600 šiqlu

… (= 1 šiqlu) = 180 ŠE

I. GLOSSARY.

1. Semitic part[1]).

א$_1$,א$_3$ל **âlum** town, *Stadt;* sometimes used as a determinative.

א$_1$ב **abum** father, *Vater;* AD(.DA)-NI = abušū his father, *sein Vater.*

Abum (waraḫ): the fifth month, *der fünfte Monat.*

א$_4$בד **abdum** servant, *Diener* (PN); probably westsemitic.

א$_2$בל **ablum** heir, *Erbe, erbberechtigter Sohn.*

abiltum heiress, *Erbin.*

ablûtum inheritance, testament, will, *Erbschaft, Testament;* ablûtam nadânum make a will, *ein Testament machen.*

א$_1$בן **abnum** stone, *Stein;* sometimes used as a determinative. TAK.ḪAR perhaps aban šewirim jewel for a ring, *Ringstein,* or compound

1) א$_1$ = arab. أ, א$_2$ = ه, א$_3$ = ح, א$_4$ = ع, א$_5$ = غ. || PN = only in proper names. || § = A. Ungnad, *Babylonisch-Assyrische Grammatik* (Munich 1906). || For the addition of *m* (mimmation) to nouns in old Babylonian see § 20a.

ideograph the value of which is not known. If TAK.ḪAR be ʿjewel for a ringʾ, TAK.ḪAR ŠU.GU and TAK.ḪAR ŠU.ŠE might designate special kinds of such jewels.

אבק **ibḳum** element in PN of uncertain meaning.

אבר$_1$ I 1: to be strong, *stark sein;* opt. lîbur (PN).

אבר$_3$ **ubârum** friend, companion, *Freund, Genosse* (PN).

אבר$_4$ **ebirtum** the opposite side of a river, *jenseitiges Ufer.*

אבר **ebûrum** harvest, *Ernte;* UD.EBUR-KU = ina (ana) ûm ebûrim.

אבת$_4$ **abuttum** mark of a slave, *Sklavenmal.*

אגר$_1$ I 1: to hire, *mieten;* praet. îgur; âgirum one who hires, *Mieter.*

אגר **ugarum** land belonging to the same town, *Feldmark.*

igarum wall, *Mauer, Wand.*

אדי$_4$ **adī** 1) praep. as far as, unto, *bis* (§ 56^{b}); 2) subj. as long as, *so lange als* (§ 61).

אדר$_1$ **Addarum** (waraḫ): the twelfth month, *der zwölfte Monat.*

אדש$_3$ **eššum,** fem. eššetum new, *neu;* MU BIL = šattum eššetum.

אוי$_3$ **awâtum** word, contents, matter, affair, *Wort, Inhalt, Sache, Angelegenheit.*

אול **awilum** man, person, *Mensch, Person;* awilum ana awilim one against the other, *einer gegen* *den andern;* m â r a w i l i m free man, *Freier.*

אוב. I 1: to leave, to draw up (a document), *lassen,
eine Urkunde ausfertigen;* praet. îz i b.

ezub except, *ausser.*

אזן. **uznum** ear, mind, *Ohr, Sinn* (PN).

אח. **aḫum** brother, *Bruder;* ŠEŠ-(A.)NI = a ḫ u š u;
pl. a ḫ ḫ ū (§ 21ᵐ); a ḫ u m ... a ḫ u m the
one ... the other, *der eine* ... *der andere.*

aḫâtum sister, *Schwester;* NIN-(A.) NI =
a ḫ â (t) z ū / a his (her) sister, *seine (ihre)
Schwester;* a ḫ â t u m ... a ḫ â t u m the one
... the other, *die eine* ... *die andere.*

אחז. I 1: to take, *nehmen;* praet. î ḫ u z.

III 1: d î n a m š û ḫ u z u m to pass judgement,
to accept a suit, *Urteil gewähren, eine Klage
zulassen.*

איכל. **êkallum** palace, *Palast.*

אין. **înum** eye, *Auge* (PN).

איר. **Ajarum** (w a r a ḫ): the second month, *der
zweite Monat.*

אכל **aklum** secretary, *Sekretär;* PA (= a k i l) SAʹL
(= sign no. 141) Š a m a š secretary of the
priestesses of Šamaš, *Sekretär der Šamaš-
Priesterinnen;* a k i l b â b d î n i m clerk at the
court of justice, *Gerichtssekretär;* a k i l t a m-
ḳ a r i m a merchant's clerk, *Kaufmannsschreiber.*

mâkaltum large it ḳ u r t u m (q. v.), *grosse* it-
ḳ u r t u m.

אל‎, **ilum** god, *Gott;* NI-NI = ì-lí my god, of the gods, *mein Gott, der Götter* (PN).

אל‎, **ul,** ulā not, *nicht* (§ 59[b]).

אלי‎, I 1: to go up, to be found, *hinaufgehen, auftauchen, sich finden;* praes. îlī; praes. illī.

I 2: to get rid of (with ina), to lose, to forfeit, *verlustig gehen.*

elûm high, lofty, *hoch, erhaben;* stat. ind. (§ 26) elī (PN); fem. elîtum in [abane]lît urṣim a precious stone, *ein Edelstein.*

אלך‎, I 1 to go, *gehen.* (PN).

אלל‎, **ellatum** strength, *Stärke.*

Elûlum (waraḫ): the sixth month, *der sechste Monat.*

אלל II 1: to purify, to set free, *reinigen, freimachen.*

ellum, fem. ellitum pure, free, *rein, frei;* stat. ind. (§ 26) ellit.

אלן‎, **Elûnum** = Elûlum.

אלף‎, **alpum** bull, *Stier;* GUD MU 3: bull of three years, *dreijähriger Stier.*

אם‎, **amtum** female slave, servant, *Sklavin, Dienerin;* a-ma-sa = *amat-šā (§ 6[lα]); amat (§ 26) she is a servant, *sie ist eine Dienerin.*

אמד‎, I 1: to lay upon, *auferlegen;* praes. im(m)id; praet. îmid; plur. îmudū (§ 5[aα]).

imdum support, *Stütze* (PN).

אמל‎, **nêmelum** possession, *Besitz* (PN).

אמם₁ **ummum** mother, *Mutter;* AMA-A.NI = ummušā.

ammatum yard, *Elle.*

ummā as follows, *folgendermassen;* ummā šunûmā thus they spoke, *so sprachen sie.*

אמק₄ **emûḳum** strength, *Stärke* (PN).

אמר₁ I 1: to see, *sehen* (PN).

אמר₃ **imêrum** donkey, *Esel;* imêr biltim pack-mule, *Lastesel.*

אן **ana** to, against, concerning (= aššum), upon, until, as, within, *zu, gegen, betreffs, auf, bis, als* (§ 56[b]).

ina in, among, during, *in, unter, während* (§ 56[b]).

אנא **uni'âtum** (plur.) furniture, *Hausgerät.*

אנב₁ **inbum** fruit, *Frucht* (PN).

אנך₁ **anakum** lead, *Blei.*

anâkū I, *ich* (§ 10).

אנן₂ **annûm** this, that, *dieser, der.*

אנן₃ I 1: to be gracious, *gnädig sein;* impv. ennam (PN).

אנש₁ **aššatum** wife, *Ehefrau;* DAM-(A.)NI =ašša(t)zū; aššat she is a wife, *sie ist Ehefrau* (§ 26).

aššûtum in aššûtum û mutûtum marriage relationship, *eheliche Gemeinschaft.*

אנת₁ **attā**, fem. attī (§ 10) thou, *du.*

אסן **isinnum** feast, *Fest.*

אפר 1 I 1: to put on (a hat), *(einen Hut) aufsetzen;* perm. apir.

אפר **eprum** food, *Speise.*

אפש **epšum** made, *gemacht;* bîtum epšum a built house, house-plot, *gebautes Haus, Hausgrundstück.*

אקל 3 **eḳlum** field, *Feld.*

ארב 6 I 1: to enter (into a house as servant or tenant), *eintreten, einziehen;* ana biltim erêbum to become taxạble, *abgabepflichtig werden;* praes. ir(r)ub; praet. îrub.

III 1: to introduce, *hineinführen.*

ארן **arnum** penalty, *Strafe.*

ארץ 1 **irṣitum** earth, *Erde* (PN).

ארץ **urṣum** a species of grain, *eine Art Getreide;* ideogr. ZAG.ḪI.LI.(S)A(R); contained in the name of the stone ^{aban}elît urṣim, v. elûm.

ארש 1 **erištum** desire, *Sehnsucht* (PN).

ארש 4 **iršum** bed, *Bett.*

ארש 5 I 1: to plant, *pflanzen;* part. êrišum in êrisa = êriš-ša (§ $6^{1\alpha}$) her planter, *ihr Pflanzer* (PN).

mêrišum plantation, *Anpflanzung.*

irrišûtum, errešûtum farming, *Bewirtschaftung.*

ארש **iršum** wise, *weise;* st. ind. (§ 26) iriš, fem. iršet (PN).

אשר **ešertum,** ešerit ten, *zehn.*

ešrîtum tithe, *Zehnt.*

aššum = an(a) šum, v. šumum.

אשת. **išten** one, *einer;* fem. išti'at.

ištiniš. one like the other, *einer wie der andere.*

אשת **ištu** 1) praep. from, *von* (. . *an*), perhaps also "at the command of", *auf Veranlassung* (4, 32); 2) subj. after, *nachdem* (§ 61).

את **ita** adjoining, *angrenzend an.*

itti with, from, at the expense of, *mit, von, auf Kosten.*

אתל. **etellum** lord, *Herr* (PN).

אתל **utlum** place at the feet of, *Gegend zu Füssen jemandes.*

אתק. III 1: to give away, *fortgeben;* IB-TA-BAL = šûtuḳ (perm.) he has given away, *er hat fortgegeben.*

אתקר **itḳurtum** a kind of dish (?), *eine Art Schüssel* (?).

ב.

בא.ל **bêlum** master, proprietor, *Herr, Besitzer.*

bêltum mistress, proprietress, *Herrin, Besitzerin.*

בב **bâbum** gate, *Tor;* bâb dînim court of justice, *Gericht;* also bâb Samaš.

בזי v. בשי.

בית **bîtum** house, house-plot, lot, *Haus, Hausgrundstück;* cf. epšum.

בכן [1] **bukânum** pestle, *Mörserkeule* (?).

בלט I 1: to live, *leben;* praes. ibaluṭ; perm. to be alive, *am Leben sein;* TI.LA-zu = balâ(ṭ)-zu.

II 1: to keep alive, *am Leben erhalten* (PN).

biltum v. ובל.

בלי **balum** without, *ohne* (§ 56c, § 57a γ) (PN).

בני I 1: to build, create, *bauen, schaffen* (PN).

בר **bûrum** offspring, *Sprössling* (PN).

ברי **birîtum** separation, *Trennung;* igar birîtim separating wall, *Trennungsmauer.*

בשי I 1: to be, exist, *sein, existieren;* praes. ibaššī; opt. libšī (PN); perm. (bašī), bazī; mala bazû as much as there is, *soviel vorhanden ist.*

bušûm something entrusted to some one, *etwas, das jemandem anvertraut ist.*

ג.

גגל **gugallum** regent, *Regent* (PN).

גלב II 1: to cut, brand, *schneiden, brandmarken.*

gallâbum barber, *Bader.*

גמל I 1: to spare, *schonen;* praet. igmil (PN).

gimillum present, *Geschenk* (PN).

גמר I 1: to accomplish, *vollenden;* perm. to have done (with), to be finished, *fertig sein.*

gamrum full, *voll;* šîmum gamrum full price, *voller Preis.*

---

1) Root very uncertain.

גנן **gannum** girdle, *Gürtel* (?).

גר **gurrum** a measure, *ein Mass.*

גשמר **gišimmarum** date-tree, *Dattelpalme.*

גשר **gušûrum** beam, *Balken.*

גתל I 1: part. gâtil (PN); read ḳâtil = קטל (to kill, *töten*)?

ד.

דאז **Du'ûzum** (waraḫ): the fourth month, *der vierte Monat* (cf. § 6c γ).

דור **dûrum** city-wall, *Stadtmauer.*

דין I 1: to carry on a lawsuit, *prozessieren;* praet. i-di-in (cf. also i-di-in = iddin; v. נדן).

dajânum judge, *Richter;* also da'ânum.

dînum lawsuit, judgment, *Prozess, Urteil;* cf. אחז₁ and bâbum.

דלל I 1: to worship, *verehren;* praes. idalal, praet. idlul (PN).

דמק II 1: to purify, beautify, *rein, schön machen* (PN).

damḳum, fem. damiḳtum, pure, beautiful, *rein, schön* (PN).

dumḳum purity, beauty, *Reinheit, Schönheit* (PN).

דקק **daḳḳum** little, *klein* (PN).

ו.

ו **û** and, also, *und, auch;* û with opt. even if, selbst wenn (cf. § 69a).

ואד,ו **wêdum** the only one, *einziger* (PN).

ובל I 1: to bring, *bringen;* praet. ûbil, ublam (PN).

I 2: to manage, *leiten, regieren* (PN).

biltum 1) burden, *Last;* cf. imêrum; 2) talent, *Talent* (= 60 manê); 3) tax, *Abgabe.*

וצא,א I 1: to come forth, move, *herausgehen, ausziehen;* praes. uṣṣē; opt. lîṣē.

III 1: to take out, *hinausführen;* ana biltim šûṣûm to rent, *mieten;* IB-TA-É(.A) = ušêṣē.

ṣîtum rising, *Aufgang;* zizzu = *ṣît-šū (PN).

mûṣûm exit, *Ausgang.*

ורד I 1: to go down, *hinabgehen;* praet. ûrid, urduma.

wardum male servant, *Sklave.*

ורח **warḫum** month, *Monat;* cf. šaddûtum.

Waraḫsamna: the eighth month, *der achte Monat.*

ורי I 1: to lead, *leiten;* perm. warī he is lead by, *er ist geleiten von* (PN).

ורך **warki** 1) praep. after (the death of), *nach (dem Tode)* (§ 56^{c}); 2) subj. after, *nachdem* (§ 61).

warkûm; fem. plur. wark(i)âtum 1) future, *Zukunft;* 2) inheritance, *Nachlass.*

ז.

זוז I 1: to divide, receive (as) a portion, *teilen, (als) Anteil erhalten;* praes. izáz, plur. izúzū;

praet. i z ú z; perm. z í z he has divided, *er hat geteilt.*

zittum portion, *Anteil.*

ח.

חבל **ḫubullum** interest, *Zinsen;* ḫ u b u l š a t t i m
yearly interest, *jährliche Zinsen.*

חגל **ḫegallum** abundance, *Überfluss* (PN).

חדי II 1: to delight, *erfreuen* (PN).

חלק I 1: to be lost, run away, *verloren gehen, weglaufen;* praet. i ḫ l i ḳ.

חנב **maḫnûbum** offspring, *Spross* (?) (PN).

חפי I 1: to destroy, annihilate, *vernichten.*
IV 1: to be destroyed, *vernichtet werden;* i - ḫ i-
p í = i ḫ ḫ i p ī.

חצר I 1: to protect, *schützen* (PN).

חרץ **ḫurâṣum** gold, *Gold.*

חתת **ḫattum** (object of) fear, *(Gegenstand der) Furcht*
(PN).

ט.

טוב II 1: to rejoice, *erfreuen;* praes. u - t a - a b - b u.
ṭâbum 1) good, *gut;* 2) satisfied, *befriedigt;*
AL-DUG = ṭ â b.

י.

יד **idum** wages, *Lohn.*

ידא I 1: to know, *wissen* (§ 53ᵍ).

יום **ûmum** day, time, *Tag, Zeit;* û m when, if, *wenn* (§ 61ᵃγ).

יצף II 1: to pay interest, *Zins zahlen;* praes. u-ṣa-ap = uṣṣap; sum. DAḪ.ḪE-DAM.

ṣiptum interest, *Zins* (is treated as if derived from צבת q. v.).

יקר **jaḳrum** dear, *teuer;* st. ind. (§ 26) já-ḳar (PN).

ירב I 1: to increase, *mehren;* praet. êrib (PN).

ישי I 1: to have, *haben;* with mimma and eli to have a claim against (upon) someone, *Anspruch haben gegen (auf) jemd.*

ישר III 2: to lead aright, *recht leiten* (PN).

išarum just, *gerecht* (PN).

mîšarum justice, *Gerechtigkeit;* mîšaram šakânum to give judgment, *Recht sprechen.*

כ.

כון I 1: to be firm, unchangeable, *fest, unwandelbar sein;* praet. ikún (PN).

II 1: to make firm, *fest machen;* praes. ukán.

kînum just, *gerecht* (PN); fixed, *festgesetzt.*

kittum truth, *Wahrheit* (PN).

כי **kîmā** 1) praep. because of, *wegen;* with the inf. "in order to", *um . . . zu;* 2) subj. because, as, in the same manner as, *weil, da, ebenso wie* (§ 61).

kî'am thus (they spoke); *so (sagten sie).*

כל **kalum** totality, *Gesamtheit;* kalušunū all of them, *sie alle* (§ 17[a]).

כלל **kilallân** both, *beide* (§ 22[a]).

כנך [1]) **kankum** sealed, stamped, *gesiegelt, gestempelt.*

kunukkum sealed document, seal-cylinder, *gesiegelte Urkunde, Siegelzylinder;* plur. ku-nu-ka-ti.

kanîkum sealed document (receipt, promissory note), *gesiegelte Urkunde (Quittung, Schuldschein).*

כס׳א **kissûm** chair, *Stuhl.*

כסלם **Kislimum** (waraḫ): the ninth month, *der neunte Monat.*

כסף **kaspum** silver, money, *Silber, Geld.*

כצר **kiṣrum** wages, rent, *Lohn, Miete;* ana kiṣrim šûṣûm (וצ׳א) to rent, *mieten.*

כר **kârum** stronghold, *Kastell.*

כרי **kirûm** garden, *Garten.*

כשד I 1: to attain, *erreichen;* dajânī kašâdum to go before the judges, *vor die Richter gehen.*

כתר v. קר׳א I 2.

ל.

ל׳א **lâ** not, *nicht.*

לאי **le'ûm** wise, *weise;* st. ind. (§ 26) le-e-i = le'ī.

לבב **libbum** heart, midst, *Herz, Mitte;* (ina) libbi in, in the midst of, *in, inmitten.*

---

1) Perhaps כנק or קנק.

לבר **labirûtum** old age, *Alter;* bâb Šamaš labirûtim the old court of justice, *der alte Gerichtshof* (?).

לבש I 1: to dress, *sich kleiden;* perm. to be clothed, *bekleidet sein.*

I 2: to clothe oneself, *sich kleiden;* il-ta-ba-aš-ši = iltabáši.

למז **lamazzum** (= lamassum) protecting deity, *Schutzgott* (PN).

לפת **liptum** work, *Werk* (PN).

nalpatum a small itḳurtum, *kleine* itḳurtum (q. v.).

לקא₃ I 1: to take, borrow, *nehmen, leihen;* with itti from, *von;* ŠU BA-AN-TI = ilḳē orilteḳē; ana mârim (or mârûtim) liḳûm to adopt, *adoptieren.*

I 2 = I 1.

milḳîtum loan, *Anleihe.*

לחת [1]) **littum** cow, *Kuh.*

מ.

מ **-mā** enclitic particle 1) used to strengthen a word (cf. ša), *dient zur Hervorhebung eines Wortes;* 2) connected with the verb (§ 32[c]): thereupon, then, in that case, *darauf, dann, in diesem Falle;* especially in conditional phrases (§ 69[a]).

---

1) Root uncertain; perhaps לא.

מא₂ר **mârum** child, son, *Kind, Sohn;* DUMU-(A.)NI = mâr(i)šū; mâr awilim free man, *Freier;* mâr bîtim (21, 20?) slave born in the house of his master, *im Hause des Herrn geborener Sklave;* mâr šiprim messenger, *Bote;* cf. also לקא₃.

mârtum daughter, *Tochter.*

mârûtum sonship, *Kindschaft,* v. לקא₃.

מגר to become favorable, *geneigt werden;* praet. imgur; dajânū ul imgurū the judges did not deem the evidence conclusive, *die Richter hielten die Zeugenaussage nicht für beweisend;* perm. to be favorable, *geneigt sein.*

I 2: to come to an understanding, *sich einigen.*

מדד I 1: to measure, *zumessen;* NI-AG-E = imadad.

מות **mûtum** death, *Tod* (PN).

muzum, read mûṣûm, v. וצא₁.

מחר I 1: to receive, *empfangen;* praet. imḫur; perm. to have received, *empfangen haben* (31, 7 maḫir wrongly instead of maḫrat).

maḫar before, *vor* (§ 56[c]).

maḫîrum market-price, *Marktpreis.*

namḫartum property, income, *Besitz, Einkommen.*

מלא₁ **malûm** full of, *voll von* (with the accus.); fem. st. ind. (§ 26; = perm.) mali'at.

malā 1) as much as, *so viel wie;* 2) praep. like, *ebenso wie.*

מלך **mâlikum** counsellor, *Ratgeber* (PN).

ממי **mamîtum** v. tûmamîtum.

מן 1) **mannum** who? *wer?* (PN).

2) **mamman** anybody, whosoever, *irgend einer, wer immer* (§ 15e).

3) **mimmā** anything, whatsoever, *irgend etwas;* mimma annîm all this, *alles dieses.*

מני I 1: to count, *zählen* (PN).

manûm mine, *Mine* (= 60 shekels).

מצי I 1: perm. to be enough, *genug sein* (PN).

מש **mâšum** twin, *Zwilling.*

משל **mišlum** half, *Hälfte.*

מת **mutum** husband, *Ehemann.*

mutûtum lit. husbandship, *Ehemannschaft;* v. aššûtum (אנש).

mâtum land, *Land.*

מתי **matī,** adī matī how long, *wie lange* (PN); matêmā for all future, *für immer.*

מתת **muttatum** forelocks, *Stirnhaar.*

נ.

נ₁אד I 1: perm. to be exalted, *erhaben sein;* read na-id (= na'id) or na-da (= nâdⁿ) (PN).

נ₂אר **nârum** canal, *Kanal.*

נב₁א I 1: to call, *rufen;* praet. i(b)bi; perm. nabī called by, *gerufen von* (PN).

נדי **nidûtum** fallowland, *Brachland.*

נדן I 1: to give, sell, *geben, verkaufen;* praes. inadin;

praet. i-di-in (= iddin; cf. דין) and idín-nam (§ 9[b]); i-na-di-iš = inadi(n)š(ī); na-di-šu = nâdi(n)šū; i-di-ši = id-(d)i(n)šī; with ana and the inf. to cause, *veranlassen*.

I 3 = I 1.

nidnum, nidintum gift, *Gabe* (PN).

nudunnûm dowry, *Mitgift*.

נור I 1: to shine, *leuchten*; opt. li-wi-ir = liw-wir (PN).

II 1: to enlighten, *erleuchten* (PN).

nawirum shining, *leuchtend* (PN).

nûrum light, *Licht* (PN).

נוח v. נסח.

נחש **nuḫšum** abundance, *Überfluss*.

ניסן [1]) **Nîsannum** (waraḫ); the first month, *der erste Monat*.

נכר II 1: to change, *ändern*.

נסח I 1: to pull out, *ausreissen*; ina aplûtim nasâḫum to disinherit, *enterben*; rugummâm nasâḫum to reject a claim, *einen Anspruch abweisen*.

נצר I 1: to protect, *schützen* (PN).

maṣṣartum deposit, *Depot*.

נש **nišū** (plur.; cf. § 18[i]) people, *Leute*.

נשא I 1: to carry, *tragen*.

---

1) Perhaps נס.א (Delitzsch).

I 2: to support, *unterstützen, pflegen;* inf. itaš-šûm (§ 38[e]).

I 3 = I 2.

nîšum elevation, *Erhebung;* nîš înim delight of the eyes, *Augenweide* (PN).

niš by the name of, *bei* (§ 56[c]).

ס.

סוק **sûkum** street, lane, *Strasse, Gasse.*

סים [1]) **Sîmânum** (warah): the third month, *der dritte Monat.*

סת **Sutûm** Sutaean, *Sutäer.*

פ.

פדי I 1: to loosen, redeem; *lösen, erlösen,* (PN).

פוק II 1: to wait for, *harren auf;* praes. upák (PN).

פות [2]) **pûtum** frontside, forehead, *Vorderseite, Stirn;* SAG-BI = pû(t)zu.

פחר II 1: to bring together, to give support, *zusammenbringen, Halt geben* (PN).

פטר I 1: to loosen, redeem, buy back, *lösen, einlösen, zurückkaufen.*

iptêrum release, *Auslösung.*

פי **pûm** mouth, word, *Mund, Wort;* ištu pê adi (or ana) hurâṣim from the mouth to

1) Root uncertain, Delitzsch סום.
2) Root uncertain.

the gold, *vom Munde bis zum Golde*, i. e. totally, *vollständig*.

פלח I 1: to honor, respect, *ehren*.

פקד **piḳittum** care, *Pflege;* pí-ḳi-ta-ša 9, 5.

פרח **pirḫum** offspring, *Spross* (PN).

פרסג **parsigum** head-cloth, *Kopftuch*.

פשר IV 1 to become appeased, *sich besänftigen* (PN).

paššûrum table, *Tisch;* paššûr ḳaḳḳadim a special kind of table, *eine besondere Art Tisch*.

פשש **piššatum** ointment, *Salböl;* pí-ša-tam 9, 4.

פת,א **teptîtum** cultivation, *Urbarmachung*.

צ.

צ,אן **ṣênū** (plur.) sheep and goats, *Kleinvieh*.

צבת **ṣubâtum** garment, *Kleid*.

ṣibtum (masc.) interest, *Zins;* ṣiptum kînum fixed interest, *fester Zins*. — The basis of the word was originally the stem יצף, but, by a popular etymology, it was connected with צבת.

צחר **ṣeḫrum**, fem. ṣeḫertum little, small, *klein*.

צלל **ṣillum** shadow, shelter, *Schatten, Schutz;* MI-NI read ṣulûli(-li) (PN).

צרר **ṣarrum** illegal, *gesetzwidrig;* stat. ind. (§ 26) ṣar.

ק.

קבא [1]) I 1: to speak, say, *sprechen, sagen;* ana gabê by request of, *auf Ersuchen*.

1) Also נבא (§ 4[d]).

I 1 = I 2.

קבל **ḳablum** midst, *Mitte;* 10, 17 probably name of an u g a r u m.

קדש **ḳadištum** female votary, *Hierodule.*

קיש I 1: to give (as a present), *schenken* (PN).

ḳîšum, ḳ î š t u m present, *Geschenk* (PN).

קמא₃ **ḳêmum** flower, *Mehl.*

קקד [1] **ḳaḳḳadum** head, *Kopf;* cf. p a š š û r u m.

קרא₁ I 1: to call, *rufen;* i ḳ - t e - r u - (u -) š i he calls (relat.) her, *er ruft sie;* others assume a root כתר to assemble, *versammeln.*

קת [2] **ḳâtum** hand, *Hand.*

ר.

ראב₃ **rêbitum** place, avenue, *Platz, breite Strasse.*

ראי₄ **rê'ûm** shepherd, *Hirt* (PN).

ראם₁ **rîmum** wild bull, *Wildstier* (PN).

ראם₃ I 1: to love, like, wish, *lieben, wünschen;* impv. r î m; with suff. r î m - a n n ī (§ 54[c]); r î m e'a n n ī (PN; 32, 1) is a wrong form due to the analogy of forms like š i m e'a n n ī.

rîmênûm merciful, *barmherzig;* stat. ind. (§ 26) r î m ê n ī (PN).

narâmum beloved one, *Liebling* (PN).

ראש₁ **rîšum** head, chief, *Haupt, Leiter* (PN).

---

1) Root originally קדקד.

2) Root uncertain.

rêštûm 1) best, *bester* (§ 28^b); NI SAG = šamnum reštûm best oil, *bestes Öl;* 2) first part, *erste Rate;* st. constr. rêštī.

רבי **rabûm,** fem. rabîtum 1) great, big, eldest (§ 28^b), *gross, ältester;* 2) rabī Amurrim (?) a title of some official, *Titel eines gewissen Beamten.*

רגם I 1: to complain, *Klage führen;* with ana 1) because of something, *wegen;* 2) against somebody, *gegen;* praes. iragam, eragam (§ 5^bα), iragum.

rugummûm claim, *Reklamation, Einspruch.*

רדי **ridûm,** fem. ridîtum heir, heiress, *Erbe, Erbin.*

רחי **terḫâtum** bridal gift, *Brautgabe.*

ריב I 1: to compensate, *ersetzen;* impv. rîb.

רכס I 1: to bind, *binden;* perm. to be bound, *gebunden werden.*

רמן **ramânum** self, *selbst* (§ 11); N. ša ramânišū N. belongs to himself, is independent, free of obligation, *N. gehört sich selbst, ist unabhängig, frei von Verpflichtung.*

רפש **rapšum** wide, *weit;* st. ind. (§ 26) rapaš (PN).

רקב **rukbum** shed, *Scheune* (?).

רשי I 1: to get, obtain, *bekommen, erhalten;* û mârī liršī-mā even if he begets children, *selbst wenn er Kinder bekommen sollte* (cf. § 69^a).

ש.

ש **ša** 1) the one of, belonging to, *der von, jemandem gehörig* (§ 13); ša N.-mā it belongs to N., *es gehört dem N.;* fem. šât (PN); used to indicate the genitive (§ 24[n]); 2) relat. (§ 16) (he) who, whoever, (*der*), *welcher, wer immer;* in oaths: that nobody, *dass niemand;* 3) subj. (§ 16[d]) that, *dass.*

שא **še'um** grain, *Getreide;* 1 ŠE perhaps = 1 ḲA še'im, but also $\frac{1}{180}$ shekel (money), 1 *ḲA Getreide, aber auch* $\frac{1}{180}$ *Sekel Geldes.*

ש.אלב **šêlibum** fox, *Fuchs* (PN).

ש.אר **šîrum** (piece of) meat, (*Stück*) *Fleisch;* 1 šîra-ta-a-an one piece of meat every time, *jedesmal ein Stück Fleisch.*

שאר **šêrum** (God of the) morning, (*Gott des*) *Morgen*(*s*) (PN).

שבט **Šabâṭum** (waraḫ): the eleventh month, *der elfte Monat.*

שגי [1]) **šaggûm** priest, *Priester.*

שדר I 1: to harrow, *eggen;* meaning not certain.

šiddum longside, *Langseite.*

šaddûtum in waraḫ šaddûtim: a designation of the harvest-month, *Beiname des Erntemonats.*

שוא **šû** he, *er* (§ 10).

---

1) Root uncertain.

שור **šewirum** 1) ring, *Ring* (cf. abnum); 2) the private money belonging to a woman, *Privatkasse einer Frau.*

שטר I 1: to write (down), *schreiben, niederschreiben;* praet. išṭur.

שיא **šî** she, *sie* (§ 10).

שיב **šîbum** witness, *Zeuge.*

שים I 1: to buy, *kaufen;* with itti from, *von;* praet. išám (cf. ŠAM).

šîmum price, value, *Preis, Wert;* ana šîmišū gamrim to its full price, *zu seinem vollen Preise.*

שים **šummā** supposing, *gesetzt* (§ 32g).

שינף [1] **šînipum** $^2/_3$.

שכך **šikkatum** ointment-box, *Salbfläschchen, Alabastron.*

שכן I 1: to place, make, found, *setzen, machen, gründen;* i-ša-ka-šu = išakanšū; cf. mîšarum (ישר).

maškanum store-house, Speicher.

שלם II 1: to keep safe, *heil erhalten* (PN).

שלש **šalšum,** fem. šaluštum third, *dritter.*

שם **šumum** 1) name, *Name;* MU-NI. IM by name, *mit Namen;* 2) posterity, *Nachkommenschaft* (PN).

aššum (orig. an(a) šum) because of, *wegen* (§ 56c).

שמ.א I 1: to hear, *hören* (PN).

---

1) Root uncertain.

שמח **šamḫum**, fem. šamuḫtum luxurious, magnificent, *üppig*, *prächtig* (PN).

šumḫum abundance, *reichliche Fülle* (PN).

šummā v. שים.

שמן **šamnum** oil, *Öl;* cf. rêštûm (ראש1).

שמר I 2: to worship, *verehren* (PN).

שן **šunū**, fem. šinā they, *sie* (§ 10).

שן **šattum** (§ 18[h]) year, *Jahr.*

שני **šanûm** second, *zweiter.*

šinā, fem. šittā two, *zwei.*

III 2: to double, *verdoppeln* (PN).

שנן I 1: to be equal, *gleichen;* lâ šanân (§ 65[e]) matchless, *unvergleichlich* (PN).

שנו **šinnum** a bronze vessel, *Bronzegefäss;* [erû]šinnu 20 ḲA a vessel containing 20 ḲA, *ein Gefäss von 20 ḲA Inhalt.*

שסי I 2: to call, *rufen.*

šisûm herald, *Herold.*

שפי **šipâtum** wool, *Wolle.*

שפר **šiprum** message, *Botschaft;* cf. mârum (מאר2).

שקל I 1: to weigh, pay, *wägen. zahlen;* praet. išḳul (= IN.NA(.AN)-LAL); praes. išaḳal (= NI-LAL-E).

I 2 in PN (ištiḳal); not quite certain.

šiḳlum shekel, *Sekel.*

שרי **Tašrîtum** (waraḫ): the seventh month, *der siebente Monat.*

שרן **šurinnum** standard, *Panier;* place where the

oath is delivered, *Ort, wo geschworen wird.*

שרר **šarrum** king, *König.*

ששן [1]) **šuššân** 1/3.

ת.

תו in **tûmamîtum** (compos.) oath, *Eid.*

תור I 1: to come back, *zurückkehren;* ul itárma ul iragam he shall not complain again, *er soll nicht wieder klagen.*

II 1: to bring (give) back, *zurückbringen, zurückgeben.*

tajârum, ta'ârum merciful, *gnädig* (PN).

tawirtum lea, meadow, *Bruch, Wiese.*

תכל I 1: to trust, *vertrauen;* also perm. (PN).

תמי I 1: to swear, *schwören;* cf. PAD.

תמקר **tamkarum** merchant, *Kaufmann.*

תן **-ta-a-an** distributive ending, *Distributivendung* (§ 57a ζ); cf. šîrum (שאר).

תנך **tannum** = nalpatum (q. v.).

תפי **tappûm** companion, *Genosse* (PN).

תפף **tuppum** tablet, document, *Tafel, Urkunde.*

תפשר **tupšarrum,** fem. tupšarratum scribe, *Schreiber;* ideograph DUB.SAR and perhaps DUMU E.DUB.BA(.A), lit. son of the tablet-house, *wörtlich: Sohn des Tafelhauses.*

---

1) Root uncertain.

2. Sumerian part [1]).

A water, *Wasser;* sem. m û.

AB verbal prefix (3. pers.), *Verbalpräfix.*

AD(.DA) father, *Vater;* sem. a b u m; AD.DA-NI = a b u š ū, AD.DA-NE.NE = a b u š u n ū.

AG to measure, *zumessen;* sem. m a d â d u m; NI-AG-E = i m a d a d.

AL verbal prefix, *Verbalpräfix;* v. DUG, TEL.

ALAM image, *Bildnis;* sem. ṣ a l m u m; ALAM-A.NI = ṣ a l a m š ū.

AMA mother, *Mutter;* sem. u m m u m; AMA-MU = u m m ī; AMA-A.NI = u m m i š ā.

A.MU.UN.NA verbal prefix (3. pers.), *Verbalpräfix.*

A.NI nominal suffix (3. pers.) *Nominalsuffix;* sem. - š ū, - š ā; cf. NI.

AZAG(.GA) pure, *rein;* sem. e l l u m.

BA verbal prefix (3. pers), *Verbalpräfix.*

BAD wall, *Mauer;* sem. d û r u m.

BAL 1) to give away, *fortgeben;* sem. š û t u ḳ u m (אתק.); IB.TA-BAL = š û t u ḳ; 2) reign, *Regierung;* sem. p a l û m.

BA.AL.LA to dig, *graben;* sem. ḫ i r û m.

BA.AN verbal prefix (3. pers.) *Verbalpräfix;* SU BA.AN-TI = i l t e ḳ ē, v. ŠU.

---

1) Arranged alphabetically.

BI nominal suffix (3. pers.), *Nominalsuffix;* sem. -šū, -šā.
BI.DA.(A.)AŠ and, *und;* sem. û; it is attached like latin -que.
BIL new, *neu;* sem. eššum.
DAḪ(.ḪE) to pay interest, *Zins zahlen;* sem. uṣṣupum (יצף); DAḪ.ḪE-DAM = uṣṣap.
DAM verbal affix (3. pers.) Verbalaffix; v. DAḪ(.ḪE).
DIB to take, *nehmen;* sem. ṣabâtum.
DI.DI to order, *befehlen;* perhaps in AB-DI.DI-NE.A.AŠ.
DINGIR god, *Gott;* sem. ilum.
DUG, good, satisfied, *gut, befriedigt;* sem. ṭâbum; AL-DUG = ṭâb.
DUMU child, *Kind;* sem. mârum; DUMU-(A.)NI = mâr(i)šū.
E affix of the present tense, *Präsensaffix;* cf. NI-LAL-E = išaḳal; NI-AG-E = imadad.
E[1]**(.A)** 1) to come forth, *herausgehen;* sem. waṣûm (יצא); IM.TA-E.A = ûṣē; 2) = šûṣûm (יצא III 1), q. v.; IB.TA-E(.A) = ušêṣē.
EGIR after, *nach;* sem. warki.
ENIM word, *Wort;* sem. awâtum; ENIM-BI = awâ(t)-zu. ENIM ŠAG.ŠAG.GA prayer, *Gebet;* sem. têmeḳum. ENIM MAL.MAL.A to complain, *Klage führen;* sem. ragâmum; ENIM NU(.UM)-MAL. MAL.A = ul iragam.
ES verbal affix of the plural, *verbales Pluraluffix* = MEŠ.

---

1) Written UD.DU.

GAL big, large, *gross;* sem. rabûm; A GAL.GAL.LA = mû rabûtum.

GAN a measure, *ein Mass.*

GE particle of the genitive, *Genitivpartikel;* GUŠKIN.GA-GE of gold, *aus Gold.*

GIM postpos. like, *wie;* sem. kîma; [d]UTU-GIM = kîma Šamaš.

GIN 1) a measure, *ein Mass;* 2) shekel, *Sekel;* sem. šiḳlum.

GI.NA fixed, *fest;* sem. kînum (כון).

GIŠ.BAR tax, measure, *Abgabe, Mass;* sem. value not known.

GU[1]) neck, bank, *Hals, Ufer;* sem. kišâdum; GU ... TA ina kišâd on the banks of, *am Ufer des.*

GUL(.LA) to destroy, *zerstören;* sem. abâtum.

GUŠKIN(.GA) gold, *Gold;* sem. ḫurâṣum.

GU.ZA (with determ. GIŠ) chair, *Stuhl;* sem. kussûm.

IB.TA verbal prefix (3. pers.), *Verbalpräfix;* v. É(.A).

ID(.DA) canal, *Kanal;* sem. nârum.

IGI.GAB(.A) to look, *blicken;* sem. naṭâlum; cf. 34, 21 (?).

IGI.RA first, *erster;* sem. ašaridum.

IM.TA verbal prefix (3. pers.), *Verbalpräfix.*

IN verbal prefix (3. pers.), *Verbalpräfix.*

IN.NA(.AN) verbal prefix (3. pers.) *Verbalpräfix.*

IN.NE.EN verbal prefix (3. pers.), *Verbalpräfix.*

IN.ŠI.IN verbal prefix (3. pers.) *Verbalpräfix.*

---

1) Written TIG.

KA particle of the genitive, *Genetivpartikel.*

KALAM.MA people, *Volk;* sem. nišū; KALAM.MA-NI-ŠU = ana nišišū.

KA.SAR wages, rent, *Lohn, Miete;* sem. kiṣrum.

KU.BABBAR silver, money, *Silber, Geld;* sem. kaspum.

LA(L) to weigh, pay, *wägen, zahlen;* sem. šaḳâlum; IN.NA(.AN)-LA(L) = išḳul; NI-LAL-E = išaḳal.

LUGAL(.E) king, *König;* sem. šarrum.

MAḪ sublime, *erhaben;* sem. ṣîrum.

MAL.MAL(.A) to make, *machen;* sem. šakânum; v. ENIM.

MA.AN verbal prefix (3. pers.) *Verbalpräfix.*

MAŠ 1) interest, *Zins;* sem. ṣibtum (צבת); MAŠ-BI = ṣiba(t)zū; MAŠ GI.NA = ṣibtum kînum; 2)?(34, 21).

MEŠ affix of the plural = EŠ.

MU 1) name, *Name;* sem. šumum; MU-NI.IM = šumšū; 2) year, *Jahr;* sem. šattum; 3) nominal suffix (1. pers.), *Nominalsuffix;* cf. AMA.

MULU man, person, *Mensch, Person;* sem. awilum.

MU.UN verbal prefix (3. pers.), *Verbalpräfix.*

NE.A.AŠ 14, 42 affix of the relative clause, *Affix im Relativsatz?*

NE.IB verbal prefix (3. pers.) *Verbalpräfix.*

NE.NE nominal suffix (3. pers. plur.), *Nominalsuffix;* sem. -šunū.

NI 1) nominal suffix (3. pers.), *Nominalsuffix;* sem. -šū; 2) verbal prefix (3. pers.), *Verbalpräfix.*

NU not, *nicht;* sem. lâ, ul; ENIM NU(.UM)-MAL.MAL.A = ul iragam; cf. ENIM.

PAD(.DE), rarely PAD.DA to swear, *schwören;* sem. tamûm; IN-PAD = itmā; IN-PAD.DE-(M)EŠ = itmû.

RA postpos. to, against, *an*, *für*, *gegen;* sem. ana.

RU(.A) to make, *machen;* sem. epêšum; sign no. 37, once no. 15.

ŠAG(.GA) heart, *Herz;* sem. libbum; ŠAG.GA-(A.)NI = libbušū.

SAG.ŠAR.RA 40, 18 of uncertain meaning.

ŠAM 1) to buy, *kaufen;* sem. šâmum (שים); IN.ŠI.IN-ŠAM = išâm; 2) price, *Preis;* sem. šîmum; ŠAM TEL.LA-BI-ŠU = ana šîmišū gamrim to its full price, *zu seinem vollen Preise.*

SI in SI... SA.SA.A to lead aright, *recht leiten;* sem. šutêšurum (ישר III 2); SI NE.IB-SA.SA.A = uštêšir(?).

SIB shepherd, *Hirt;* sem. rê'ûm.

SU 1) hand, *Hand;* sem. ḳâtum; ŠU... TI to take, borrow, *nehmen, leihen;* sem. liḳûm (I 1, I 2); ŠU BA.AN-TI = il(te)ḳē. 2) written KU; postpos. to, for, *zu, für;* sem. ana; KA.SAR MU 1 KAM ŠU = ana kiṣir šattim išti'at.

SUM to give, *geben;* sem. nadânum; MA.AN-SUM = idinnam (PN).

ŠU.NIR standard, *Panier;* sem. šurinnum; ŠU.NIR GAL.GAL.LA = šurinnū rabûtum.

SU.SILIM.MA 14, 42 of uncertain meaning.

TA postpos. at, in, of, *an, in, von;* sem. ina, ištu; GUŠKIN-TA of gold, *aus Gold.*

TEL(.LA) 1) to be finished, *fertig sein;* sem. גמר (perm.); AL-TEL = gamir; 2) full, *voll;* sem. gamrum; cf. ŠAM.

TI v. ŠU.

TI(L), TI.LA to keep alive, *am Leben erhalten* (PN); sem. uballiṭ.

TU.RA to bring in, dedicate, *hineinschaffen, weihen;* sem. šûrubum (ארב, III 1.).

U (written UD) day, *Tag;* sem. ûmum; U-KUR-ŠU = ana matêmā, q. v.

UŠ, usually UŠ.SA in MU UŠ(.SA) following year, *folgendes Jahr.*

ZI.BI.EŠ 40, 17 of uncertain meaning.

II. LIST OF PROPER NAMES.

ARRANGED ALPHABETICALLY.

NB. š and ṣ have been inserted after s, ṭ after t, ḳ after k. — Abbreviations: *m.* = masculine personal name; *f.* = feminine personal name; *t.* = name of a town; *tpl.* = name of a temple; *c.* = name of a canal.

Aabba *m.*
Aa-ḫegal *c.*
Aa-šitī *f.*
Aa-tallik *f.*
Abba-ṭâbum *m.*
Abdum *m.*
Abi-ešuḫ *m.*
Abijatum *m.*
Abil-ilišū *m.*
Abil-Sin *m.*
Abu(m)-w(j)aḳar *m.*
Abunum *m.*
Adâ *m.*
Adajatum *m.*
Adī-anniam *m.*
Adī-matī-ilī *m.*
Aḫam-neršī *m.*
Aḫâtânī *f.*
Aḫattum *f.*
Aḫâtum *f.*
Aḫujatum *m.*
Aḫunī *m.*
Aḫušinā *m.* (3, 9 perhaps not proper name).
Ajatija *f.*
Akija *m.*
Akilama *m.*
Akkadûm *t.*

Bunini-abī *m.*

Bûr-Nunu *m.*

Bûr-Rammân *m.*

Bûr-Sin *m.*

Bûrtânī *f.*

Buzatum *m.*

Dabîtum *f.*

Daḳḳum *m.*

Damiḳtum *f.*

Da-šeg (?) *t.* (27, 24).

Dili-ilum (-Anum ?) *m.*; not certain.

DUMU-NIN.ḪAR.SAG.GA *m.*

Dûr-mûti *t.*

Ea-ḫegal *m.*

Ea-idinnam *m.*

Ea-mudamiḳ *m.*

Ea-na'id *m.*; perhaps to be read Ea-nâda.

Ebarbarram-lûmur *m.*

Ebarbarrum *tpl.*

Êbirum *m.*

E.ḪE *tpl.*

E.KI.BI.GI (= Bîtam-ana-ašrišū-têr) *m.*

Elī-êrisā *f.*

Ellil-abī *m.*

Ellil-abum *m.*

Ellil-ilum *m.*

Ellil-nâdin-šumi *m.*

Ellurum *m.*

E.ME.TE.UR.SAG *tpl.*

E.NAM.TI.LA *m.*

EN.KI-MA.AN.SUM (=Ea-idinnam) *m.*

Ennam-ilī *m.*

Ennam-Sin *m.*

Ennam-Šamaš *m.*

Êribam *m.*

Êrib-Sin *m.*

Erištī-Aa *f.*

Erištī-Šamaš *f.*

Erištum *f.*

E.TEL.AN.NA *tpl.*

E.TEL.AN.NA-MA.AN.SUM (?) *m.*

Etellum *m.*

Etel-pî-Nabi'um *m.*

Etel-pî-UR.RA *m.*

E.UL.MAŠ *tpl.*

Gablum name (?) of an *ugarum*; perhaps not proper name (= *ḳablum ?*).

Gagum *t.*

Ga'ilatum *f.*

Gâmilum *m.*
Gaminânum *t.* (?)
Gimil-Marduk *m.*
Gimil-NIN.SUN *m.*; perhaps ŠU-NIN.SUN.
Gizânu name (?) of an *ugarum;* perhaps not proper name.
Ḫabil-kînu *m.*
Ḫajatum *m.*
Ḫalijatum *f.*
Ḫam(m)ū-rabī *m.*
Ḫappatum *m.*
Ḫarirum *m.*
Ḫilur *m.*; uncertain.
Ḫumurum *m.*
Ḫunâbija *f.*
Ibaluṭ *m.*
Ibgatum *m.*
Ibija *m.*
Ibī-NIN.ŠAḪ *m.*
Ibī-Ša'an *m.*
Ibḳu-Aa *m.*
Ibḳu-Annunitum *m.*
Ibḳu-Antum *m.*
Ibḳu-ilišū *m.*
Ibḳu-Išḫara *m.*
Ibḳu-Ištar *m.*
Ibḳum *m.*
Ibḳu-Nabi'um *m.*
Ibḳu-Nâr-Irnina *m.*
Ibḳušā *m.*
Ibḳu-Samaš *m.*
Iblê *t.* (?)
Ibnī-Amurrum *m.*
Ibnī-Ellil *m.*
Ibnī-Rammân *m.*
Ibnī-SAK.KUD (NIN.IB) *m.*
Ibnī-Šamaš *m.*
Ibnī-Tišḫu *m.*
Ibnī-Urra *m.*
Idadum *m.*
Idin-Ellil *m.*
Idinja *m.*
Idin-MA.MU *m.*
Idin-Nunu *m.*
Idin-Sin *m.*
Idin-Šamaš *m.*
Igmilum *m.*
Ikatum *m.*
Ikûn-pî-Sin *m.*
Ikûn-pîšā *m.*
Ilī-dumḳī *f.*
Ilī-êribam *m.*
Ilī-gimlannī *m.*
Ilī-imnannī *m.*
Ilī-ištiḳal *m.*

Ilī-itê *m.*
Ilîmā-aḫī *m.*
Ilī-mâlikkī *m.*
Ilîmā-ta'âr *m.*
Ilī-matī *m.*
Ilī-rîmeannī *m.*
Ilī-tappišū *m.*
Ilumā *m.*
Ilum(Anum?)-abī *m.*
Ilum(Anum?)-idin *m.*
Ilum(Anum?)-imanum-gama *m.*; very uncertain.
Ilum(Anum?)-lamsigâ *m.* very uncertain.
Ilum(Anum?)-mâlik *m.*
Ilum(Annm?)-mušalim *m.*
Ilum(Anum?)-pî-Aa *m.*
Ilum(Anum?)-pî-Sin *m.*
Ilum(Anum?)-rabī *m.*
Ilum(Anum?)-šemē *m.*
Ilušū-abušū *m.*
Ilušū-bânī *m.*
Ilušū-ella(t)zū *m.*
Ilušū-ibi(šū) *m.*
Ilušū-ibnī *m.*
Ilušū-nâṣir *m.*
Imdī-Ellil *m.*
Imguja *m.*
Imgur-Ea *m.*
Imgur-Kêš *m.*
Imgurrum *m.*
Imgur-Sin *m.*
Ina-ḳâti-Šamaš *m.*
Ina-libbim-iršet *f.*
Inbum *m.*
Innabatum *f.*
Ipṭur-Sin *m.*
Isî *m.*
Isin(na) *t.*
Išarum *m.*
Iškun-Marduk *t.*
Išmē-Sin *m.*
Ištar-ummī *f.*
Išum-gâmil *m.*
Išum-nâṣir *m.*
Itti-Ea *m.*
Izamanum *m.*
Izigatar *m.*
Jadiḫ-el *m.*
Jagab-el *m.*
Jaḳub-el *m.*
Jaḳubu(m) *m.*
Jaḫḳub-el *m.*
Japsû *m.*
Japuš *m.*
Kalkatum *m.*

Karanatum *f*.
KA'-ša-Kêš *m*.
KA'-ša-NIN.TU *m*.
KA'-ša-Nunu *m*.
KA'-ša-Šamaš *m*.
Kêš-gâmil *m*.
Kinišzuma *m*.; very uncertain.
Kišušû *m*.
Kittum-ṣulûlī *m*.
Kunatum v. Manatum.
Kurkudum *m*.
Kurkurum *m*.
Ḳiš-Nunu *m*.
Ḳišti-Ea *m*.
ḲU [1])-Ištar *m*.
Laḫutum *m*.
Lamazī *f*,
Lazarura *m*.
Lîburam *m*.
Lîbur-nâdišū *m*.
Lipit-Ellil *m*.
Lipit-Ištar *m*.
Lišimurum *t*.
Luḫutum *m*.; uncertain.
Luštamar-Sin *m*.

Maḫnub-ilim *m*.
Majatum *f*.
Makula *m*.; very uncertain.
Manatum *m*.; perhaps to be read Ḳunatum.
Maninum *m*.
Man(n)um-balum-ilim *m*.
Mannum-ibaššī-bêlanū *m*.
Manum *m*.
Marduk-lamazašū *m*.
Marduk-mušalim *m*.
Marduk-tajâr *m*.
Mâr-irṣitim *m*.
Mâr-NIN.ḪAR.SAG.GA *m*.; v. DUMU.
Mâr-Sippar *m*.
Mâr-Šamaš *m*.
Maṣiam-ilī *m*.
Mâšum *m*.
Matatum *f*.
Meranaki *m*.; uncertain.
MER.RA ... or Rammânra ... *m*. 4, 20; very uncertain.
Milkī-itti-ilija *m*.
Mîšarum-bânī *m*.

1) The tablet has not GAZ; ḲU and GAZ have sometimes the same meaning.

Muḫaddîtum *f.*
MULU-NANNA(R) *m.*
Munawirtum *f.*
Munawirum *m.*
Mupaḫirum *m.*
Mutablum *m.*
Nabī-ilišū *m.*
Nabī-Sin *m.*
Nabī-Šamaš *m.*
Nab(p)ritum *f.*
Naḫimum *m.*
Nakarum *m.*
Nakimum *m.*
Namram-šêrum *m.*
NANNA(R)-AZAG.GA *m.*
NANNA(R)-IGI.RA *m.*
NANNA(R)-MA.AN.SUM *m.*
NANNA(R)-MULU.TI(L) *m.*
Nanum *m.*
Narâm-ilišū *m.*
Nâr-Ḫammurabī *c.*
Nâr-Irnina *c.*
Nâr-Samsuilunā *c.*
Nêmelum *m.*
Nidadum v. Idadum.
Nidintum *f.*
Nidnat-Sin *m.*
Nidnušā *m.*
NIN.A.ZU *f.*
NIN.GIR-abī *m.*
NINNI-AMA-MU *f.*
NIN.ŠAḪ-MA.AN.SUM *m.*
Nîši-înišū *f.*
Nûratum *m.*
Nûr-Ea *m.*
Nûrija *m.*
Nûr-ilišū *m.*
Nûr-KAB.TA *m.*
Nûr-Marduk *m.*
Nûr-Sin *m.*
Nûr-Šamaš *m.*
Nûrum *m.*
Nutubtum *f.*
Paka-ila *m.*; uncertain.
Palatum *f.*
Pirḫi-ilišū *m.*
Piri-Aa *m.*; read Wari-Aa.
Pûḫânum *m.*
Purattum Euphrates.
Puṭur-Sin *m.*
Rabâtum *f.*
Rammân-bânī *m.*
Rammân-idinnam *m.*
Rammân-lâ-šanân *m.*

Rammân-ra . . . cf. MER. RA . . .
Rammân-rabī *m.*
Rammân-rîmênī *m.*
Rapaš-ṣilli-Ea *m.*
Rībam-ilī *m.*
Rîbatum *f.*
Rîb-Nunu *m.*
Rîš-Šamaš *m.*
Salimatum *f.*
Samamum *m.*
Samsu-ilunā *m.*
Samu-la-el v. Sumu-la-el.
Sanatam *m.*; uncertain.
Sapatum *m.*
Sililum *m.*; cf. Zililum.
Sin-abušū *m.*
Sin-adalal *m.*
Sin-aḫam-idinnam *m.*
Sinatum *m.*; cf. Zinatum.
Sin-bânī *m.*
Sin-bêl-abli(m) *m.*
Sin-bêl-ilī *m.*
Sin-ella(t)s(z)ū *m.*
Sin-ennam *m.*
Sin-êriba(m) *m.*
Sin-gâmil *m.*
Sin-ḫattī *m.*
Sin-idinnam *m.*
Sin-ilum *m.*
Sin-iḳîšam *m.*
Sin-imgur(r)annī *f.*
Sin-išme'an(n)ī *m.*
Sin-jatum (= Sijjatum) *m.*
Sin-ḳâšid *m.*
Sin-le'ī *m.*
Sin-ludlul *m.*
Sin-magir *m.*
Sin-mubaliṭ *m.*
Sin-mušalim *m.*
Sin-nâdin-šumi *m.*
Sin-nâṣir *m.*
Sin-pidîmā *m.*
Sin-puṭram *m.*
Sin-rîmênī *m.*
Sîn-rîm-Urim *m.*
Sin-tappi-wêdi *m.*
Sin-ublam *m.*
Sippar *t.*
Sugagum *m.*; also Zugagum.
Sumuja *m.*
Sumu-la-el *m.*
Sumu-ramê *m.*
Ša-ilišū *m.*
Ša-Išḫara *m.*
Šamaja *m.*

Šamaš-abilšunū *m*.
Šamaš-abušū *m*.
Šamaš-balâ(ṭ)zū *m*.
Šamaš-bânī *m*.
Šamaš-da'ân *m*.
Šamaš-emûḳī *m*.
Šamaš-gâmil *m*.
Šamaš-gâtil *m*.
Šamaš-GU *m*.; uncertain.
Šamaš-gugal *m*.; uncertain.
Šamaš-ḫâṣirum *m*.
Šamaš-ḫegal *m*.
Šamaš-ilum *m*.
Šamaš-în(a)-mâtim *m*.
Šamaš-iris (? 24 , 9) *m*.; uncertain.
Šamaš-kâšid *m*.
Šamaš-liwir *m*.
Šamaš-magir *m*.
Šamaš-MA.AN.SUM, v. UTU.
Šamaš-muštêšir *m*.
Šamaš-mutabilšunū *m*.
Šamaš-napšeram *m*.
Šamaš-nâṣir *m*.
Šamaš-nûrī *f*.
Šamaš-rabī *m*.
Šamaš-rê'ī *m*.
Šamaš-rîš *m*.; reading uncertain.
Šamaš-šemī *m*.
Šamaš-ṣulûlī *m*.
Šamaš-tajâr *m*.
Šamaš-tappišu *m*.
Šamuḫtum *f*.
Šât-Aa *f*.
Šelibu *m*.
Šeritum *m*.
Šêrum-bânī *m*.
Šilânum *m*.
Šubna-el *m*.
Šummā-ilum(-Anum?) *m*.
Šumuḫ-Sin *m*.
Šumu(m)-libšī *m*.
Šumum-lîṣē *m*.
Ṣabi'um *m*.
Ṣabi'um-ilum *m*.
Ṣil(l)i-Ištar *m*.
Ṣil(l)i-NIN.KAR.RA *m*.
Ṣil(l)i-Rammân *m*.
Ṣil(l)i-Šamaš *m*.
Ṣiz(z)ū-na(wi)rat *m*.
Tabgiri-Šamaš *m*.
Takumatum *f*.
Tamlatum *m*.; reading not certain.

Tarâm-Akkadâm *f.*
Ṭarâm-UL.MAŠ *f.*
Taribatum *f.*
Taribum *m.*
Taškun-Ištar *t.*
Tišit-Ellil *c.*
Tupliaš a district near Elam.
Turukum 31, 14.
TU.TU-ḪE.GAL *c.*
Ṭâbija *m.*
Ṭâbum name (?) of an *ugarum*; perhaps not proper name.
Ṭâb-Urum *m.*
Ubar-NIN.IB *m.*
Ubarrija *m.*
Ubarrum *m.*
Ubar-Šamaš *m.*
UL.MAŠ v. E.UL.MAŠ.
Ummī-Araḫtum *f.*
Ummī-Išḫara *f.*
Ummī-ṭâbat *f.*
Upâḳum *m.*
Urkîtum-lamazī *f.*
UR.RA-bânī *m.*
UR.RA-gâmil *m.*
UR.RA-nâṣir *m.*
Uruk *t.*
Urum *t.*
Uštašnī-ilum(-Anum?) *m.*
Utul-Ištar *m.*
UTU-MA.AN.SUM *m.*
UTU-ŠU-MU.UN.DIB *m.*
Warad-Amurrim *m.*
Warad-Ellil *m.*
Warad-ilišū *m.*
Warad-Išḫara *m.*
Warad-Ištar *m.*
Warad-kubi *m.*
Warad-Nunu *m.*
Warad-Rammân *m.*
Warad-Sin *m.*
Warad-Šamaš *m.*
Wardum *m.*
Warī-Aa *m.*; cf. Piri-Aa.
Zaban (or Zaman?) *t.*
Zabbum *m.*
Zaniḳ-gabê *m.*
Zarikum *m.*
Zikilaja *m.*
Zilakum *c.*
Zililum *m.*; cf. Sililum.
Zinatum *m.*; cf. Sinatum.
Zizzū-na(wi)rat v. Ṣ.

Zugagum *m.*; also Sugagum.

Zuḫâ name (?) of an *ugarum;* perhaps not proper name.

Zû-ila *m.*

ADDITIONS AND CORRECTIONS.

p. XI, l. 8. Quite recently a treatise on old Babylonian legal documents has appeared by W. Hazuka. (*Beiträge aus den altbabylonischen Rechtsurkunden zur Erklärung des Hammurabi-Kodex.* Teil I. [Berlin thesis] 1907).

Note that in the Sign-List (*a*) in accordance with the transcription adopted in the glossary, ḳ is to be substituted for q, and (*b*) that to save space the mimmation is omitted.

p. 44, no. 86 add: GIŠ.LIŠ.GAL = *ismâkaltu*,
GIŠ.LIŠ.TUR = *isnalpatu* or *istannu*.

p. 46, no. 137: to KI.UD add *maškanu.*

p. 47, no. 176: read IŠKUR instead of MER; (the same in the List of Proper Names p. 37[b], l. 22 and p. 39[a], l. 1).

Glossary.

p. 1. In accordance with the author's grammar, י has been transcribed by *j*, not *y*; for the difference between ^ and ¯ over a vowel cf. § 3[k].

p. 4, l. 20 read: bull, three years old, instead of: bull of three years.

p. 13, l. 4 read כנך instead of כנך.

www.ingramcontent.com/pod-product-compliance
Lightning Source LLC
Chambersburg PA
CBHW070605180626
46817CB00005B/2002
9781606083819